Enduring

Desire

Your Guide to Lifelong Intimacy

Michael E. Metz
Barry W. McCarthy

Routledge
Taylor & Francis Group
New York   London

Routledge
Taylor & Francis Group
270 Madison Avenue
New York, NY 10016

Routledge
Taylor & Francis Group
27 Church Road
Hove, East Sussex BN3 2FA

Printed in the United States of America on acid-free paper
10 9 8 7 6 5 4 3 2 1

International Standard Book Number: 978-0-415-87830-2 (Paperback)

Library of Congress Cataloging-in-Publication Data

Metz, Michael E.
    Enduring desire : your guide to lifelong intimacy / Michael E. Metz & Barry W. McCarthy. -- 1st ed.
      p. cm.
      Includes bibliographical references (p.   ).
    ISBN 978-0-415-87830-2 (pbk. : alk. paper)
    1. Intimacy (Psychology) 2. Interpersonal relations. I. McCarthy, Barry W., 1943- II. Title.

BF575.I5M48 2010
306.77--dc22

2010021217

Visit the Taylor & Francis Web site at
http://www.taylorandfrancis.com

and the Routledge Web site at
http://www.routledgementalhealth.com

To my spouse, Hildy Bowbeer, for her strong and enduring support.

To all the women and men, clergy, healthcare, media, and teaching professionals who are promoting positive, healthy, "good enough" couple sexuality as a strong energy in their real lives.

Michael Metz

To my grandsons Torren Michael McCarthy and Liam Karl McCarthy, and my granddaughter Daphne Jeannette McCarthy, with the hope that they grow up in a world that celebrates healthy male, female, and couple sexuality.

Barry McCarthy

Contents

Acknowledgments

This book represents what we have learned in our combined 75 years as clinical psychologists, sex and marital therapists, and researchers. We are especially indebted to our clients, students, and professional colleagues who have taught us so much and added to the quality of the material in this book.

We want to acknowledge and thank the outstanding contributions of the publishing team at Routledge/Taylor & Francis, especially our esteemed and wise editor, Dr. George Zimmar—his support of this book has been unusually robust; his attentive and efficient editorial assistant, Marta Moldvai; our conscientious copyeditor, Joanne Freeman; Julia Gardiner for energetic marketing; and Judith Simon, for careful editorial production. Our thanks and deep appreciation.

Introduction

You'll never read another book about sex and intimacy like this one!

Why? We don't just help you enjoy pleasurable and great relationship sex. We promote realistic, positive sexual expectations without commercialism and the exotic hype that sets you up for disappointment. We will not misrepresent or overpromise. We will not sell you products or magic techniques "guaranteed" to cure every sex problem. Rather, we'll give you straight talk about realistic, high-quality, affirming, exciting, smile-inducing, warm, wild, comforting, and enduring sexual pleasure. We'll encourage you to strive for lifelong desire and optimal sexual satisfaction. We'll motivate you with real-life examples and clear, helpful individual and couple exercises. We'll describe the value of emphasizing desire, pleasure, and eroticism. It is important to develop your couple sexual style—including conflict resolution, playfulness, and integrating sex into your real life. Our ultimate goal is to guide you to greater couple intimacy and realistic sexual joy. Our message is down to earth and full of satisfaction for couples from their twenties to their eighties.

This book will help you explore the essential features of sexual intimacy, desire, and satisfaction that are sustaining and joyful amid the stresses and challenges of real life. Couple sex offers a strong source of energy that helps individuals and couples live life well. You want your sex life to contribute a generous amount of the motivation and energy needed to celebrate your love, as well as sometimes simply get you through the day. Rather than sex being a problem or distraction in your daily life, it deserves to be a reliable, consistent source of desire, pleasure, eroticism, and connection with your partner, providing comfort and solace for life's stressors and a vital energy to embrace the challenges of life.

The fact that our book caught your attention verifies that you've got what it takes: you positively value sex and are interested in enhancing your sex life. On the other hand, you may doubt your partner's satisfaction, or feel dissatisfied yourself: "Is that all there is?" Maybe you worry about maintaining satisfaction as you grow older? Or perhaps you don't have a current relationship and wonder if there is something problematic about your sexual approach. We will help you successfully confront these issues with self-confidence.

This book can and will revolutionize your intimate life. In it, we examine the different meanings of "quality" sex and propose a new model of exceptional sexual quality that is relevant for men, women, and couples at every age. We directly challenge the "Perfect-Sex" and "Perfect Intercourse" models with our "Good Enough Sex" (GES) model for lasting and lifelong couple sexual satisfaction. You'll learn how to "think right" about quality couple sex and to understand why the prevailing beliefs about "perfect sex" are toxic. Our "Good Enough Sex" concept and lifestyle is not a cop-out; it's a roadmap to a lifetime of terrific, meaningful sex, a guide to help you feel sexually satisfied, not in a fantasy world but in real life. Sexual satisfaction is fundamentally grounded on realistic physical, psychological, and relationship expectations. Unrealistic expectations precipitate frustration, distress, and a sense of failure. GES lays out the basics of a truly satisfying sex life. We are sure you won't be disappointed; rather, you'll be relieved, affirmed, and inspired to consider the honest truth about how to have great sex at every stage in your life.

WE'RE EXCITED ABOUT THIS BOOK!

This is the most exciting, earnest, and challenging book project that the authors have joined forces to write. We have a real "passion" for this book and its message for couples wanting a vibrant sex life while coping with the activities and demands of everyday existence. We have published numerous articles on couple sexuality and the GES model in professional journals (e.g., Metz & McCarthy, 2007; McCarthy & Metz, 2008; Metz & McCarthy, 2008). With strong encouragement from our professional colleagues (e.g., "the public *really* needs your approach"), and amazing feedback from our clinic patients, we felt this was the time to share this cutting-edge scientific and clinically relevant material with you, the reading public.

WHO WE ARE AND WHY WE WROTE THIS BOOK

Both authors are Ph.D. clinical psychologists, as well as marital and sex therapists. This is our fourth co-authored book, but the first written specifically for both individuals and couples. Michael Metz practices individual, couple, and sex therapy in Minneapolis/ St. Paul, and previously was on the faculty of the University of Minnesota Medical School for 12 years. Barry McCarthy practices in Washington, DC, and is a professor of psychology at American University. Between us we have nearly 70 years of clinical experience working with individuals and couples, and have presented more than 400 professional workshops on topics involving relationships and sexuality.

Our motivation in writing *Enduring Desire* is to:

- Guide real couples to increase their happiness by promoting a positive and vital sex life.
- Help individuals and couples set positive, realistic sexual expectations that encourage the growth of sexual satisfaction.
- Prevent sexual problems and foster adaption to normal sex difficulties.

As we clinically treat couples mired in the blame, shame, and demoralization caused by sexual problems, we are aware that many of these situations could have been prevented, or at least more easily alleviated, if the couple had access to affirming attitudes about sex; confident psychosexual skills and scenarios; were comfortable with their bodies, pleasure, and eroticism; and had developed positive, realistic sexual expectations amid the challenges and changes of life. Knowledge is power. We hope to empower you as individuals and as a couple to understand, integrate, and value the strategies of GES so that you can enjoy life-long desire and exceptional-quality couple sexuality throughout your lives.

HOW TO USE AND BENEFIT FROM THIS BOOK

The book begins with Chapter 1's overview of an innovative and realistic way of thinking about your sexuality and Chapter 2 lays out the GES "growth goals" for quality couple sex. The chapters that follow explore in detail each of the ten GES guidelines. Case illustrations serve as examples, and exercises help you fully appreciate how each feature is essential to a vibrant, healthy sexual relationship. You and your partner can focus on chapters that are personally relevant and speak to your strengths, as well as areas of sexual vulnerability to address and change. Our book will help you see the larger picture and also recognize personally significant goals to pursue to ensure your lifelong sexual satisfaction.

We suggest you be an active learner rather than just a passive reader. For example, you could read aloud to each other, or one of you could underline personally relevant points in orange, the other in blue, and then discuss these important points over a cup of coffee or a glass of wine. Our mantra for change is:

1. Read together
2. Talk together
3. Do together

The "growth goals" of our GES model are the core components for achieving excellent and satisfying sex throughout your life. If you ignore one of these features, you risk diminishing your pleasure and satisfaction. Compare them with the common notions of a "perfect relationship" with "perfect sex" prevalent in our society today and recognize how different this book is in exploring quality couple intimacy and sexuality. Rather than emphasizing your insecurities and fears of inadequacy, we invite you to challenge the fallacies that you're somehow lacking and that everyone else has great sex, ideas that you haven't challenged for all the wrong reasons—e.g., penis/breasts too small, hair not right, deodorant didn't work as well as advertised, overweight, muscle tone not super, wrinkles a turn-off. Instead of needless worry, you'll learn to be open to new, healthy ways of thinking that will enhance your pleasure and guide your sexual growth in the years ahead.

Let's begin!

1

Real Sex for Couples
The New Way of Thinking

Why are so many people unhappy with their sex lives? Does it seem to you that nearly everyone else has great sex compared to you? Is anyone really satisfied or is sexual satisfaction such a moving target it seems unattainable? Does anyone over 30 have great sex? And why is sex so important? Too often people chase great sex in the wrong directions and listen to the wrong sources. Great sex is not magically found in a pill, although sometimes chemistry can help. Great sex is not primarily found by making yourself "beautiful" or "handsome," although that can help too. Great sex is not automatic or found by "fortune."

Mark Twain's remark many years ago seems very true today—especially about sex: "The problem isn't that people know too little, but that people know too much that just ain't so." Do you "know too much that just ain't so?" Test yourself about what you "know" about quality sex by completing the following quiz:

Quiz: What You Know About Quality Sex

Yes _____ No _____	Sexual satisfaction depends on the frequency of orgasm for both men and women.
Yes _____ No _____	Can you have erectile dysfunction and still feel sexually and emotionally satisfied?
Yes _____ No _____	Being overweight is an automatic barrier to great sex.

1

Yes _____ No _____ Sexual quality is best in the first 2 years of a relationship.

Yes _____ No _____ Pornography illustrates great sex.

Yes _____ No _____ Religion is a major cause of poor-quality sex.

Yes _____ No _____ Sexual affairs are omnipresent.

Yes _____ No _____ Sexual experimentation (e.g., anal intercourse) is essential for sexual quality.

Yes _____ No _____ Sex declines in long-term couples.

Yes _____ No _____ Penis size is a major factor in sexual quality and satisfaction.

Yes _____ No _____ Quality sex in ensured by a serious, analytic approach to lovemaking.

Yes _____ No _____ Having children inevitably undermines couple sex.

Yes _____ No _____ Couples must make their sex life the number one priority.

Yes _____ No _____ For a couple to have quality sex, the responsibility rests with the woman.

Yes _____ No _____ Sex satisfaction ultimately depends on sexual performance.

Yes _____ No _____ Physical illness and disability inevitably destroy quality sex.

Yes _____ No _____ Quality couple sex is impossible for persons who have been sexually abused.

Yes _____ No _____ Women's sexual satisfaction is always helped by breast implants.

Yes _____ No _____ Because women and men differ so much sexually, quality sex is only for one or the other.

Yes _____ No _____ Young couples enjoy the best quality sex.

Yes _____ No _____ Sexual quality depends on the woman maintaining her youthful beauty.

Yes _____ No _____ Great sex requires daily sex.

Yes _____ No _____ Raw physical sex is the best sex.

Yes _____ No _____ In satisfying relationships, the frequency of orgasm is the same for men and women.

Yes _____ No _____ Satisfied couples always have love as their sexual goal.

This is a couple sex-myth test. According to the best research and professional experience, all of these items are "no" or false. In the chapters to follow, we'll guide you to understand the facts, but more important, we'll teach you how to build attitudes, feelings, and behaviors that ensure your sexual and emotional relationship will continue to flourish and be all it can be.

It is very difficult to get accurate, meaningful information about intimacy and quality sex. This book will help you do that. Our message is that sex is natural and healthy and can contribute to your overall enjoyment and happiness with life regardless of age. Developing positive attitudes, psychosexual skills, and emotional expressiveness is important, and varies for each couple. In a real way, molding satisfying couple sexual intimacy is a special "do-it-yourself" project that brings challenges and joys at every age and stage of your relationship.

BUILD ON WHAT YOU ALREADY HAVE FOR LIFELONG SEXUAL SATISFACTION

Whether you are in your 20s, 40s, or 60s, the ten sexual growth features presented in Chapter 2 will affirm what is already healthy in your relationship and describe how to ensure optimal quality sex in the future. This includes:

- Cooperating with your partner as an "intimate team" to provide a healthy climate for quality sex;
- Optimizing your comfort and confidence with sex;
- Feeling proud of your sexual self and sexual relationship;
- Understanding your body's need for relaxation to enhance pleasure;
- Balancing pleasure with sexual function;
- Accepting variable, flexible sexual desire and experiences;
- Ensuring comfort and confidence by realizing that sex has multiple purposes and arousal styles;
- Affirming that sex can fit into and enhance your life with playfulness and special feelings.

Understanding these features inoculates you against sexual dysfunction and other sexual problems.

HEALTHY THINKING ABOUT SEX

Of course, we want fantastic, incredible, "great" sex all the time, spontaneously and everywhere—sex that just blows your mind! We want to ride the wave of excitement, soar like the eagle, and become delirious. And we want to instantly escape the humdrum pace of everyday life, feel intensely connected to that moment of ecstasy. This makes for a great sex fantasy but not real-life quality sex.

The fantasy approach to sex leads to thoughts such as:

- I must be missing out because I don't have great sex like I see in movies. What's wrong?
- My sex life is routine, even mediocre at times; it's second-rate, pretty much the same all the time, uninspiring, dull.
- I feel that everybody else has much better sex than I.
- Don't we love each other anymore?

Such thoughts are common. Accept that we all have these or a variety of other satisfaction-sapping ponderings. Our innovative way of regarding sex will help you develop healthier, realistic sexual thinking that will enhance your pleasure and satisfaction. Pursuit of "perfect sex" is natural, like the surfer who seeks the perfect wave. Yet we would do well to appreciate that riding the perfect wave is relative to riding and appreciating the ordinary waves. Without the variation, even the "perfect" wave is boring. Sex is enhanced by appreciating its healthy variability. Researchers (Kleinplatz, Menard, Paradis, Campbell, Dalgleish, Segovia, & Davis, 2005) have learned from older couples that optimal, exceptional sex experiences and lackluster ones exist in the same relationship. Mature couples can find great pleasure, solace, eroticism and intimacy with their bodies.

SEEKING QUALITY COUPLE SEX

Our new way of thinking about and approaching quality couple sex will seem peculiar at first, but read on. With our ten guidelines for sexual growth, you will develop an enduring quality of erotic sex that is gratifying, sustaining, and self- and

Our "Good Enough Sex" (GES) model is the best approach for real couples.

partner-satisfying. We call this approach to real-couple sex, the "Good-Enough Sex" (GES) model, which seeks optimal sexual experiences based on a realistic appreciation that variations over time are healthy and necessary. Otherwise we set ourselves up for disappointment and disillusionment.

GOOD-ENOUGH SEX? YOU'VE GOT TO BE KIDDING!

Are you thinking, "Good Enough Sex? Get out of here! You've gotta be joking!" We can imagine what your first reaction is since we hear it often—the incredulity of settling for sex that is "mediocre," "boring," "get-by," "mechanical," and other lackluster notions. But not so; hear us out.

This "good-enough" concept emerges from a long tradition in psychology (e.g., Winnicott, 1964), which explains that concepts of happiness, satisfaction, and contentment are built on what Dr. Paul Dormont (2009) calls "relative nirvana"—the happiness of striving for growth blended with acceptance of real-life limitations, imperfections, and the diversity of human experience.

The GES we're talking about is *realistically great sex* that serves a number of purposes in your life—pleasure, tension release, self-esteem, emotional intimacy, and/or reproduction. We're talking real people with real lives with real responsibilities and pressures, real kids, and demanding jobs. We're talking real sex that fits into real life and, reciprocally, real life that fits into your sex life with enduring desire and satisfaction.

The GES approach is based on the nearly 70 years of professional sex therapy, serious relationship and sex research, and the clinical experience of seasoned marital and sex therapists. We developed the GES model as a positive set of principles for long-term, committed couples who experience sex dysfunction. This model guides therapists in their creative design of sex therapy interventions to help distressed couples and facilitates couple reflection on the meaning and value of their sexual relationship. We soon discovered that these positive principles have wide appeal and are relevant to healthy couples who want to enhance intimacy and sexuality.

The GES approach is consistent with and supported by recent research advances in the area of well-being known as "Positive Psychology" (e.g., Seligman, Rashid, & Parks, 2006; Lent, 2004). The GES model emphasizes how positive dimensions of couple sexuality can promote aspects of happiness (e.g., Lyubomirsky Sheldon, & Schkade, 2005). This research corroborates that when you are (1) realistic and genuine; and (2) constructive and affirmative about life's experiences, including sex, you are happier. This research proposes that we have a lot to say about our own happiness. Do you think your happiness is in your power? A choice you make? We do, and we want you and your partner to be happy and satisfied with your relationship, including sex.

In the GES model, self-understanding and sexual meaning are crucial. Sex is not viewed as an isolated fragment of your life; rather, it is integrated into your individual and couple daily life, as daily life is integrated into your sex life. Your daily life provides the opportunity to enrich sexual interactions in a subtle yet distinctively personalized way.

KEEP PERSPECTIVE

Do not get hijacked by words that over-promise and set up impossible and self-defeating expectations for sex. Don't fall victim to marketing hype like "orgasms that last for hours" or "ecstasy every time." To think you can

> The "Good-Enough Sex" (GES) guidelines advance your optimal couple sexual satisfaction while realistically blending healthy variations in quality.

have perfect sex every time in any circumstances is pure hype. No one has a perfect sex life. Hype sets you up for self-defeating performance demands and disappointment. Get real! Instead think: really good sex, enduring desire, realistically satisfying, high-quality, and genuine couple sex—sex that provides a positive energy and that most days gives support to your daily life. Sex provides a buffet of experiences: at times, sex is enthusiastic, cheerful, erotic, gratifying and at other times uninspiring.

Real sex can be experienced as pleasing, eager, impulsive, affectionate, tender, passionate, mechanical, intimate, warm, reassuring, distracted, joyful, enchanting, amusing, gleeful, lackluster, fulfilling, comforting, delightful, thrilling, affirming, contented, harmonious, playful. "Great" sex, especially in a committed relationship, is uneven and variable. What the best research suggests is that regular frequency and variable, flexible couple sex that is fully integrated into your real life is the best quality, most satisfying, wonderful sex for you as a couple.

IS GES RIGHT FOR YOU?

We'll help you to *think* in a sexually healthy manner throughout the stages and adaptations in your life. We'll show you how to *act* in a sexually healthy way to build a lasting and satisfying couple sexual bond. We'll guide you to *feel* sexually satisfied, not in a fantasy world but in real life.

We don't want to sound like we're dispensing more hype, but judge for yourself whether our GES approach for enduring desire and sexual satisfaction is right for you. Consider what we've learned from our many years of combined experience as relationship and sex therapists, researchers, teachers, and group facilitators. By embracing the ideas laid out in our book, you have little to lose and a lifetime of solid sexual satisfaction to gain.

We explore how real couple sex works and how to have smile-on-your-face sex that is honest and wonderfully satisfying. We'll explain how great sex actually grows and matures, and how to fashion an "intimate team" with your partner to integrate sexual pleasure and security into your real lives. Fast-moving, intense, demanding lives are not barriers to healthy sex, but rather situations in which you can find exquisite pleasures, joys, affirmation, acceptance, fun—even when distracted and exhausted from the responsibilities of contemporary living.

WE OFFER YOU REALISTIC CONFIDENCE

Our new model of exceptional sexual quality is relevant for women, men, and couples, whether married or in a serious relationship. Age is irrelevant. We write about sexuality for real-life couples, not for the perfect, beautiful, stereotyped couples who are portrayed in movies and music videos. Throughout this book, we will confront "sexual hype" that supposedly liberates you but instead intimidates you and makes sex a performance test in which you have to prove something to your partner or to yourself.

This book aims not to intimidate you but to empower you as individuals and as a couple. The cultural hype about sex creates dysfunction, dissatisfaction, and disillusionment. For example, R-rated movies show young, beautiful couples either in a new relationship or an extra-marital affair. They are in a highly desirous state before any touching begins. Arousal is extremely rapid and high, and everyone is multi-orgasmic. Great fantasy and entertainment, but exactly the wrong model for real-life couples. We tell our sex therapy couples that if you have Hollywood-type sex once a month you are doing better than 95% of the population.

The core of quality couple sexuality is a *biopsychosocial* (body, mind, relationship), *multidimensional* (thoughts, feelings, behaviors), *comprehensive* (multiple perspectives) understanding of the roles, functions, and meanings of couple sexuality, as well as the value of vital passion, intercourse, and orgasm. The new mantra for healthy, lifelong couple sexuality is desire, pleasure, eroticism, and satisfaction as an intimate team.

WHAT YOU NEED TO KNOW TO DEVELOP
AND MAINTAIN QUALITY COUPLE SEX

Your role is to actively and calmly engage in setting personally relevant goals and work as an intimate team to promote lifelong quality couple sexuality. First, you need to realize that long-term satisfying sex is built and vitalized in a healthy cooperative relationship, what we call your "intimate team." Second, you need to know that sex is not simple or automatic—unless maybe for procreation. Quality sex and satisfaction are growth processes. We develop physical, psychological, and relationship satisfaction gradually and progressively. If you are a younger person, look ahead with confidence to enjoying integrated sexual pleasures and satisfaction in your future. With dedication, sex can become qualitatively better and lasting. Research studies report the best quality sex occurs in couples who have been in a committed relationship for 15 years or longer (Laumann et al., 1994). Yes, hard to believe, but accurate. And an example of how prevailing hype and misinformation that sex is best among young couples give us misdirected, even toxic, advice.

BASIC INGREDIENTS OF SEXUAL SATISFACTION

In the chapters that follow, we explain the ten GES growth goals for lifelong sexual satisfaction. This approach to better understanding the dimensions of quality couple sex is known professionally as an "integrative" approach (see Figure 1.1). This means that for thorough understanding, you continuously blend the five dimensions of yourselves and your relationship. You appreciate (1) that sex is a lifelong growth process "developmental," (2) the importance of your body ("biological"), (3) your thoughts, behaviors, and feelings ("psychological"), (4) your interactions ("social/ relational"), and (5) the skills involved for sexual satisfaction ("psychosexual").

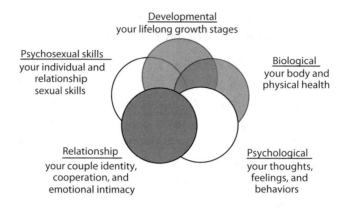

Figure 1.1 Sexual health and satisfaction.

The *Developmental* feature reminds you that your sexual health is a lifelong undertaking involving learning, growing, discovering, and integrating features of your sexual health. Each life stage offers special joys and challenges.

The *Biological* element includes your body and the physiologic dimensions of sex: vascular, neurologic, hormonal and lifestyle dimensions (e.g., alcohol usage, physical condition, smoking).

The *Psychological* dimension involves your thoughts or cognitions, actions or behaviors, and your emotions or feelings such as comfort and confidence.

Relationship features consist of (1) your couple "identity" involving each partner's expectations of sex, level of relationship cohesion versus individual autonomy, gender roles; (2) cooperation and level of mutual conflict resolution; as well as (3) intimacy, especially mutual empathy.

Psychosexual Skills include cognitive, emotional and behavioral lovemaking skills. These encompass the three basic sexual arousal styles, couple sexual pleasuring skills, kinds of touch, erotic scenarios, intercourse scenarios, and flexible techniques.

ENDURING DESIRE

This integrative understanding guides you to appreciate the complexity of sexual desire and satisfaction. Too many believe that over the lifecycle, sexual desire and satisfaction are diminished. The reality is that sexuality becomes more integrated for healthy couples.

> Your sexuality will develop and mature when you commit to our GES approach.

When younger couples believe that desire for and quality of sex will inevitably decline, this becomes a self-fulfilling prophecy. This results from viewing sex as one-dimensional, as being merely physical and that sex inevitably declines after we reach our physical peak (ages 18–25). This notion itself is a trap. Realize that while your body may developmentally mellow, your psychological and relational desires and joys mature and deepen. Quality sex is physical but, more significant, it is also psychological and interpersonal. Adult couples do appreciate this, but are reserved. They don't get on TV and proclaim, "We have wonderful experiences of sex; it is better than ever." *Enduring Desire* is your guide to sexual satisfaction throughout your relationship. Appreciate that your sexuality will develop and ripen when you commit to the features of our GES approach.

THE GES APPROACH: COGNITIVE, BEHAVIORAL, EMOTIONAL, AND COUPLE FEATURES

Features that characterize the GES model include cognitive, behavioral, emotional, and relational factors that promote couple cohesion, cooperation, and intimacy. Examples of *cognitive* dimensions include a positive attitude toward sex, taking personal responsibility for pursuing developmental ("lifelong") sexual growth, and a commitment to mutual sexual health. *Emotional* features include accepting and caringly expressing your honest feelings about sex and distinguishing feelings from behaviors. *Behaviorally*, as a couple you cultivate cooperation to ground your sexual pleasure on physical relaxation. You also learn healthy psychosexual skills such as flexibility, regularity, as well as partner interaction, sensual self-entrancement, and role enactment arousal styles. Crucially important is that you function as an "intimate team," prioritize emotional empathy, forgive each other for prior disappointments, and view your sexuality as an essential relationship forum and opportunity for cohesion.

YOUR THOUGHTS ARE IMPORTANT FOR SATISFACTION

When it comes to understanding sexual satisfaction, the psychological dimensions—how we think (cognitions), what we do (behaviors), and how we feel (emotions)—are all essential, intertwined ingredients (Figure 1.2).

Your cognitions or thoughts are premier (Epstein & Baucom, 2002). They facilitate your emotions, and these feelings tell you how satisfied you are with your sex life. The thoughts, feelings,

> Your sexual expectations are crucial.

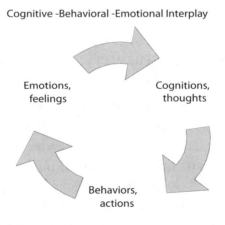

Cognitive -Behavioral -Emotional Interplay

Emotions, feelings

Cognitions, thoughts

Behaviors, actions

Figure 1.2 Cognitive-Behavioral-Emotional Interplay.

and experiences in your extended, nonsexual lives are powerful influences, but it is your sexual cognitions that are crucial. This is why we emphasize accurate and reasonable expectations.

If you think sex should always be exceptional and do not realize the normal variability of couple sex, you set up unattainable goals. When sex falters, you make negative attributions such as, "Our sex life is poor so we're in trouble." "We're falling out of love." "Our relationship is flawed." Or, we hold unreasonable beliefs like "I should always excite him." "A real man always has automatic erections." Then when ordinary erectile problems occur, he mis-attributes it: "Because I can't perform, I've failed my partner." Or, consider the unreasonable belief that "the woman should have an orgasm every time," so that when she doesn't, it sets up common misattributions such as "I'm a failure." Or "she's frigid."

Often these negative thoughts automatically operate in the background of our minds as self-evident "truths," reinforced by the social hype about sex. The GES principles help you to challenge such cognitive mistakes, which create feelings of anxiety, self-doubt, inadequacy, and low self-esteem—all based on unreasonable expectations. The way you think about sex itself, its role in your lives and relationship, and your expectations are crucial. While thoughts, behaviors, and feelings automatically interact, your cognitions or thoughts are most important in determining the meaning sex has for you. *The meaning to you and your partner is at the core of your relationship and sexual satisfaction.*

CHOOSE WHAT IS RIGHT FOR YOU AND YOUR RELATIONSHIP

To understand quality couple sex, you cannot compare yourself to some idealistic model. There is no simple formula that applies to all couples. Rather, GES offers the core features that make up realistic quality couple sex that you integrate into your unique relationship. This allows you to discuss and choose what is right for you as a unique couple. What would support your couple sexuality so it is comfortable, functional, vibrant, erotic, and satisfying? We can't say it often enough: Knowledge is power. You want to make wise choices that work emotionally and practically, both short and long term.

CRUCIAL POINTS FOR SATISFYING SEX

Sexual satisfaction involves how you think about sex, how you feel about your body and your lovemaking, and the quality of your intimate relationship:

- Sex is important *at any age*. Don't let yourself think otherwise. You are a sexual person, capable of satisfying sex until you die. Biologically, what benefits your physical body also benefits your sexual body. The good news is that illness does not stop you from being sexual. You can enjoy sex into your 60s, 70s, and 80s. Being healthy—especially following good sleep patterns, exercising regularly, and eating well—promotes sexual health.
- A common feature of couples who have a strong, vibrant, and pleasurable sex life is that they *maintain a "regular" sexual connection*. This means a steady pattern of sex regardless of what barriers may arise. Research verifies the value of regularity, whether twice a week or three times a month. When you know your pattern, good things happen.
- Satisfaction with your sexual life is fundamentally grounded *on accurate knowledge*—realistic physical, psychological, and relationship expectations. Unrealistic expectations precipitate frustration, distress, and a sense of failure.
- A very valuable guideline is to *define sexuality as mutual pleasure* rather than intercourse. Too many couples get into the pattern of "intercourse or nothing." Defining sex as intercourse is an extremely risky, self-defeating

approach because ultimately you will have ignored the all-important mind-body element of sexuality.

- *Appreciate the importance of promoting desire* as a core component in healthy sexuality. Biological factors (with the exception of hormonal disorders) seldom directly affect desire. What does affect desire is illness, medication side-effects, fatigue, and unresolved couple conflict. These increase anticipatory anxiety, performance anxiety, self-consciousness, and resentment, which interfere with positive anticipation—the core element in sexual desire.

- *Psychosexual skills* refer to your comfort and skill with scenarios and techniques to build sexual anticipation and receptivity. These include playfulness, relaxation, pleasuring, erotic scenarios, cooperative intercourse, and comfort with afterplay scenarios that enhance sexual satisfaction. Among the topics we'll explore are the three basic styles of sexual arousal and their importance for lifelong sexual function and satisfaction.

- *Adopt the new mantra of quality couple sexuality*: desire, pleasure, eroticism, and satisfaction.

ACCEPTANCE FOR SEXUAL SATISFACTION

These core principles support sexual satisfaction. Satisfaction involves feeling happiness or pleasure: "I feel good" or "I feel satisfied with my relationship." Dissatisfaction feels disappointed, sad, or alienated. Many believe that their feelings are "automatic" and result directly from the situation. In fact, it is crucial to understand the interconnection between our feelings, behaviors, and thoughts. Ultimately our relationship and sexual satisfaction rests on the *emotional* dimension (i.e., feeling good, satisfied) that is grounded in the *cognitive* dimension (i.e., positive thoughts) and played out in the *behavioral* dimension (such as how well we cooperate, function, share as individuals and as a couple).

How we think is the crucial feature in sexual desire and satisfaction. Satisfaction involves acknowledging great erotic experiences, pleasurable and functional sexual encounters, sex encounters that are good for one partner but not the other, encounters that are more intimate than sexual, functional but mediocre encounters, and even dysfunctional encounters. A crucial dimension of the GES model is to stay on the same intimate team whether the encounter is fabulous or a "bomb." Couples grounded in reality accept variability and enjoy the entire range of desire, pleasure, eroticism, and satisfaction.

SUMMARY

The GES approach introduces a new way of thinking about, experiencing, and emotionally valuing quality couple sexuality. The new mantra for quality couple sexuality, whether married or in a serious relationship, whether you are 20 or 80, is to develop a mutually comfortable level of intimacy, value pleasuring, integrate erotic scenarios and techniques, and establish positive, realistic sexual expectations as an intimate team. In the following chapters we will be describing in detail the variable, flexible GES model, which emphasizes desire, pleasure, eroticism, and satisfaction. We will present exercises, case studies, and a tool-box of skills to help you integrate these concepts into your couple sexual style.

2

Your Growth Goals for Quality Sex

Real life is a journey to embrace.

Anonymous

HEALTHY SEX HAS JOYS AT EVERY AGE

Understanding the essential features of lifelong quality couple sex helps you set your sexual "growth goals." You might already be comfortable and confident with some features; others will be a challenge to pursue and master.

Satisfying couple sex differs from one encounter to the next, and from age to age. There are special enjoyments, delights, and satisfaction at every age. Sexual quality varies throughout life; it's different for younger, midlife, and older couples. Sexuality can play a valued part in life at whatever stage we are living. The 25-year-old couple can enjoy quality sex that emphasizes youth and vitality, while the 40-year-old and 70-year-old couples enjoy distinguishing qualities specific to their maturity and life situation. Circumstances also influence sexual quality. Sex for a single person looking for a life partner is different than for a married couple with children, an older couple with the freedom of retirement, or a lively couple in their 80s, together for 60 years.

Younger couples typically share more acrobatic sexual interactions than 80-year-old couples, although the pleasures for each can be expansive. Sexual pleasure and satisfaction has special joys at every age.

YOUR UNIQUE RELATIONSHIP

There is not one path to sexual quality. Healthy and satisfying sex is something you uniquely create with your intimate partner.

> **Healthy sex is supported by smart thinking, cooperation, emotional intimacy, and eroticism.**

Your sexual style will be similar to others but it will have special and distinctive qualities. The truth is that quality sex is not luck, a mystery, or an undeserved bonus. "Great sex" is built little by little, has its ups and downs, and deepens over time—strengthened by the vicissitudes of real life. Quality couple sex is a growth process. It is absolutely true that "sex gets better with age," like fine wine. This is not an easy concept to grasp, but when younger couples approach their sex life with this awareness, it encourages them to appreciate the quality they currently enjoy, gives vision for ensuring quality sex, and inoculates them from sex problems in the future. Viewing your sex life in this light puts you on a path for optimal sex throughout your relationship.

QUALITY COUPLE SEXUALITY CHANGES AND GROWS

If you are a couple who feels you have a high level of sexual satisfaction, that is great, but you cannot rest on your laurels. Life will bring you new experiences and challenges. Life does not endorse permanent stability, in spite of our longing for it. The moment you feel you've "arrived," life will remind you there's more. One hallmark of life is that "change is inevitable." Healthy sexuality embraces this constant change, adapts to it, savors the moments of stability, and celebrates life's challenges and shifting dimensions.

Most couples begin as a romantic love/passionate sex/idealized relationship. This is a very important phase because it gives you the courage to take the risk and become involved in a serious relationship. However, by its nature, this is a fragile, short-lived phase, usually lasting 6 months to a year, seldom more than 2 years. The challenge for serious couples, whether married or unmarried, is to integrate intimacy and eroticism into their relationship. The good things in life require attention and effort.

YOUR LIFELONG SEXUAL GROWTH GOALS

There are a number of elements or "growth goals" that characterize quality sex throughout life. Sexual quality is a developmental process. Contrary to cultural myth, sexual satisfaction does not peak in youth and is not diminished by children, careers, and other responsibilities. While the sexual quality of youth is vibrant and often quite satisfying, it is only the "first phase" of expansive quality and satisfaction. It is important for younger couples to be aware of this potential or be at risk of falling into the negative, self-fulfilling prophecy that supposes "sexual satisfaction inevitably declines."

Lifelong sexual satisfaction is hard for most people to believe—especially couples inundated with the stereotypic impressions formed by movies, commercial promotions, and the general media.

The reality is that stable and vital relationships are characterized by enduring and satisfying sex, which deepens throughout the years. This is ensured when you work together to build a sex life that provides regular energy in your relationship and learn to stay focused on pleasure, cooperation, and mutual empathy—shaped by adapting

> While the sexual quality of youth is vibrant and often quite satisfying, it is only the "first phase" of expansive quality and satisfaction.

to life's successes and trials. Living life experiences as an intimate team *expands and deepens your sexual satisfaction.*

TEN FEATURES OF LIFELONG SATISFYING SEX

When you have positive, realistic "growth goals," the effort to achieve healthy and satisfying sex is not burdensome. Inspired by clear purpose, you and your partner can readily follow a growth process. Your growth goals patiently and generously become your unique relationship's "mission statement" for vital, strong couple sex.

> **GES is your blueprint for quality sex.**

Table 2.1 presents the ten essential features of enduring quality sex—the elements of "GES." These are the features that promote lifelong quality couple sex. GES is your blueprint for quality sex. We discuss each feature in detail in the chapters that follow.

Features that promote the GES model include cognitive, behavioral, emotional, and relational factors that reinforce cohesion, cooperation, and intimacy. Examples of the cognitive dimension include developing and maintaining a positive attitude toward sex, taking personal responsibility for pursuing developmental (lifelong) sexual growth, and ensuring a deep commitment to mutual sexual health.

Emotional dimensions include accepting your honest feelings about sex and your body, and distinguishing feelings from behaviors.

Behaviorally, cultivate sexual desire and emotional self-regulation, ground your sexual pleasure on physical relaxation, and learn sensual self-entrancement and role enactment arousal.

Especially important is that you cooperate as an intimate team, prioritizing mutual emotional empathy (Jacobson & Christensen, 1998), forgiving each other for prior disappointments (Spring, 2004), and viewing your sexuality as an essential component of your relationship and a special opportunity to integrate intimacy and eroticism.

Healthy women and men intentionally foster understanding of each other, celebrate similarities, accept and adapt to differences, and integrate these into their sexual relationship throughout life.

Some of the GES guidelines offered are easy, some are surprising, and some are challenging. Some make intuitive sense, while others seem "off the wall." Your puzzlement is reasonable because if each feature were automatic, everyone would pursue healthy sex spontaneously and there would be no reason for you to grow as

Table 2.1 Ten Growth Goals for GES

Commit yourself to pursuing the following ten lifelong sexual quality goals:

1. Value sex as a good element in your life—an invaluable part of your individual and couple comfort, intimacy, pleasure, and confidence.
2. Commit yourself to ensuring that sex is satisfying at every age and every stage in your life. Sexuality develops, grows, and evolves throughout your life.
3. Ground your sex satisfaction on realistic, age-appropriate sexual expectations. Accurate and reasonable knowledge about sexual physiology, psychology, and relationship health are crucial for sexual satisfaction.
4. Remember that sexuality is inherently relational. You want to grow as an intimate team. Create your own couple sexual style—complementary, traditional, soul mate, or emotionally expressive. Sexual health and satisfaction are directly influenced by the quality of relationship identity and conflict resolution, which mold emotional and sexual intimacy.
5. Value each other's sexual body and practice good physical and psychological health, which is vital for your sexual health. Celebrate with your bodies.
6. Accept that there is no right or wrong way to be sexual. Respect, value, and integrate your individual and gender differences. Cooperate for sexual satisfaction.
7. Value sensual touch and its pleasurable feelings, as well as intercourse and orgasm. Satisfied couples keep in mind that relaxation is the foundation for sensual pleasure and sexual function.
8. Understand that sexual and relationship quality varies. Abandon the "need" for perfect performance and instead value variable, flexible sexual experiences. Integrate the five basic reasons for sex, flexibly use the three sexual arousal styles, and develop flexible alternatives to intercourse.
9. Integrate your real life into sex and sex into your real life to create and nurture your distinctively personalized, unique sexual relationship.
10. Personalize sex and celebrate passion. Sex can be playful, spiritual, and "special." Occasional playfulness facilitates "special" sex, which is characterized by acceptance, trust, pleasure, and vitality.

---

sexual individuals and a couple. Quality sex would be a "done deal." Of course, this is an unrealistic expectation.

OVERVIEW OF THE PRINCIPLES FOR REAL SEX FOR HEALTHY COUPLES

Think of the items listed in Table 2.1, designed to foster your sexual relationship. When you live the GES approach, you cooperate as a couple to value sex as a genuine, intimate connection. View this as a progressive, lifelong process complete with joys and sorrows as you endeavor to adapt and grow at each stage of your lives. In following the GES guidelines, you recognize, accept, and adapt to career stresses, family crises and losses, and parenting and financial successes and worries. You integrate these life happenings into your relationship and sexual experiences.

- Paramount to satisfaction at every stage is grounding your relationship and sexual expectations on reality. Consciously defy the hype and imbalanced commercial marketing of sex. Search out honest, scientifically valid information about sexuality. Value and trust your sexual experiences, read scientifically grounded books and trusted articles on sexuality, and adjust your expectations of sexual function and practices based on accurate knowledge and your own comfort and preferences.
- Appreciate that your sexuality is inherently relational. While retaining your individual sexuality, strive to become an "intimate team." Your overall relationship is energized by your team identity, cooperation to resolve conflicts, and emotional intimacy. Sexual intimacy is energized by desire, arousal, orgasm, and satisfaction—qualities that warrant your ongoing attention and cooperation.
- For lifelong sexual vitality, practice good physical and psychological health, especially in regard to adequate sleep, exercise, and diet. Value each other's sexual bodies

as sources for pleasure and eroticism, as well as comfort and acceptance.

- A hallmark of sexually healthy couples is respect for your partner's individual differences. The man comes to deeply appreciate the woman's personal and sexual feelings. The woman comes to deeply respect the man's personal and sexual feelings. Celebrate your differences, and tolerate what is less positive. For example, a man affirms and generously accommodates the woman's experience of her menstrual cycle and menopause, while the woman affirms and generously accommodates his sexual drive. Couples who blend gender differences feel respected, accepted, and proud of their relationship.

- The psychosexual skills involved in GES form the foundation for exceptionally satisfying sexual quality. These features ensure sexual pleasure, immunize the partners against sexual dysfunction, invite deepening emotional intimacy, and increase sexual desire, passion, and vitality. At the core of sexual function—as counterintuitive as it appears—is physical relaxation. Two basic features influence sexual function: physiological relaxation and sufficient physical and psychological stimulation. Satisfied couples value sensual touch and emotional connection as well as sexual function and orgasm.

- Couples not only accept, but also affirm that sexual quality *varies* from one experience to another. It is normal and healthy that on occasion a sexual encounter is better for one partner than the other. Sometimes an encounter is emotionally satisfying, but not erotically satisfying, and vice versa. Some encounters are very special and others are unremarkable. Even dissatisfying or dysfunctional encounters can have some level of satisfaction if you are able to shrug them off as normal couple variability and make a date to be sexual in the next few days. You can enjoy the peaks and smile at the valleys of sexual function/

dysfunction and satisfaction/dissatisfaction. This understanding provides a "bigger picture" of your intimate life, rather than allowing satisfaction to ride solely on this one encounter. While affirming sexual variability, you can embrace the GES approach and adopt several tools to understand and influence couple sex. For example, realizing there are multiple reasons to be sexual and that there are three basic arousal styles can help you adapt to the unpredictability of sexual experiences. Such knowledge helps you comfortably cooperate as an "intimate team."

- Sexually healthy couples personalize their passion and lovemaking. Ensure that your sexual connections are "regular." That is, you can count on sex not in a hit-or-miss fashion, but as an integral part of your relationship. This is one of the features that distinguishes quality sex and ensures enduring satisfaction. This aspect is very important because when challenging circumstances occur in your life, you must bring sex into your real life, come "hell or high water." Personalize your sex, making it a consoling pleasure amid crises, playfulness at another time, and as a transcendental or spiritual experience at other times. Healthy sex is characterized by emotional trust, pleasure, acceptance of real life, and vitality.

Use the next exercises to examine priorities in your relationship, as well as define your sexual growth goals in the weeks, months, and years ahead.

· · · · · · ·

EXERCISE 2.1 AFFIRMING YOUR STRENGTHS AND SETTING YOUR GES GROWTH GOALS

Individually review the 10 guidelines in Table 2.1 and rate your strengths. Rate the power of your "Current Strength" for each dimension by assessing each on a scale of 1 to 10, with 10 meaning a "very strong strength" and 1 meaning a "very fragile strength."

Then rate "Your Desired Priority for Growth" for each dimension by assessing each on a scale of 1-10, with 10 meaning "very strong desire" and 1 to meaning "very low desire."

Share these ratings with your partner: Discuss similarities and differences for your "Current Strength" ratings and "Desired Priority for Growth" ratings. Items that you agree on are your valued strengths, which reinforce your sexual relationship. Those on which you have discord are potential growth areas to set as goals for your future.

Finally, together rank order "Your Priority Decisions as a Couple" for the three most important growth goals, with 1 representing your top priority, 2 your second priority, and 3 your third priority. Clarifying these three areas is important in enhancing your relationship and sexual satisfaction and working as an intimate team.

The Ten GES Lifelong Growth Goals	Rate Your Current Strengths (1–10)	Your Desired Priorities for Growth (1–10)	Your Priority Decisions as a Couple (up to 3)
1. Value sex as a good and positive element in your life.			
2. Commit to sex being satisfying at every age.			
3. Ground your sexual satisfaction on realistic, age-appropriate relationship and sexual expectations.			
4. Commit to creating your own couple sexual style.			
5. Celebrate each other's sexual body; engage in good physical health practices.			
6. Respect, value, and integrate your individual and gender differences.			
7. Value sensual touch for pleasure as well as sexual function.			
8. Accept that sexual and relationship quality varies.			

(Continued)

(Continued)

The Ten GES Lifelong Growth Goals	Rate Your Current Strengths (1–10)	Your Desired Priorities for Growth (1–10)	Your Priority Decisions as a Couple (up to 3)
9. Ensure regular sex and integrate your real life into sex and sex into your real life.			
10. Personalize sex as playful, spiritual, and special.			

Exercise 2.2 helps you set specific sexual growth goals.

• • • • • • •

EXERCISE 2.2 CLARIFYING YOUR GOALS FOR SEXUAL SATISFACTION

You are unique in your sexuality as a couple. This exercise asks you to assess your current sexual relationship and establish specific sexual growth goals. You can implement growth goals as you explore concepts, strategies, and techniques throughout this book. We ask you to first do this separately and then discuss your ratings with your partner. Assess four dimensions of sexuality and utilize two time frames. The four dimensions are:

1. *Desire: This means anticipation of being sexual and feeling that you deserve to have sexuality be a positive force in your relationship.*
2. *Arousal: How objectively aroused (in terms of vaginal lubrication and erection) as well as subjectively aroused (feeling "turned on") are you?*
3. *Orgasm: Does high arousal naturally flow to orgasm (climax) that is neither premature nor inhibited? How often do you want to experience climax?*
4. *Satisfaction: At the end of a sexual encounter, do you feel better about yourself, and more bonded and energized as a couple?*

Assess each of these four dimensions in two time frames: (a) when it was most satisfying and (b) how each dimension functions and feels at present.

Remember, don't try to impress your partner, "fake it," or judge yourself by a perfect sex performance standard. Be honest with yourself and your partner about sexual strengths and vulnerabilities.

From this base of honest assessment of sexual function and feelings, set positive, realistic individual and couple sexual growth goals for the next year. Be clear with yourself and your partner in setting personally relevant goals, rather than "hype" goals. For example, a personally relevant goal would be to increase pleasure and enjoy being the giving partner; a "hype" goal would be to be the sexiest couple in your community. A personally relevant goal for the woman might be to increase subjective arousal and on occasion request afterplay stimulation to orgasm; the "hype" goal would be to have "G-spot" orgasms or be multi-orgasmic each time. A realistic goal for the man would be to ask his partner's help with psychosexual skill exercises to improve ejaculatory control so that intercourse lasts between 2 and 7 minutes; the "hype" goal would be for intercourse to last 20 minutes so your partner is orgasmic each time.

In terms of sexual growth goals, remember the mantra of GES: desire, pleasure, and satisfaction.

Appreciate your strengths as a couple and learn how to promote your individual and relationship growth goals to increase sexual satisfaction.

SUMMARY

Quality couple sex is totally different than the hyped sex seen in R-rated movies or porn videos. The prime emphasis is on individual and couple acceptance and setting positive, realistic sexual expectations based on biological, psychological, and relational realities.

As you consider personally relevant couple growth goals, you have an opportunity to incorporate the variable, flexible GES features with their emphasis on positive, realistic expectations and to build your unique couple style to serve as the basis for lifelong quality couple sexuality.

3

Your Expectations and Sexual Satisfaction

The concept of GES challenges you to set positive, realistic expectations about your sexual bodies, as well as your psychological and relationship dimensions. Our society is saturated with images and myths about beauty and manliness, sexual performance, and an over-emphasis on romantic, perfectionistic sexuality. Healthy couples realize that their bodies have age-appropriate capacities. They view sexuality as a lifelong developmental process that involves changes and differences from young adulthood to older age, and adapt their expectations to each life phase.

APPRECIATE THAT HYPE AND COMMERCIALISM MISLEAD YOU

Media advertisements exaggerate sexual reality for marketing purposes. Wise couples deal with this by valuing their personal experience and by seeking scientifically accurate knowledge from trusted websites and/or books. For example, sexual science reports that periodic sexual problems are common, sexual enjoyment varies, orgasm is not essential to sexual satisfaction, and men and women have different physiological and psychological experiences. Hype and exaggerated claims that seem "too good to be true" inevitably are.

EVERY COUPLE HAS SEX DIFFICULTIES

Most couples are amazed to learn the scientific facts about sexual function and dysfunction. While studies consistently report frequent sexual dysfunction among 40% to 50% of couples at any given time (Laumann, Gagnon, Michael, Michaels, 1994), an even greater percent (78%–95%) indicate common sexual difficulties (Frank, Anderson, & Rubenstein, 1978; Metz & Seifert, 1993). For example, partners complain of disagreements over sexual frequency, styles, preferred behaviors (self-pleasuring, oral sex, sexual variety), amount of partner interaction, experiences with sexual boredom, and hypersensitivity to their sexual partner. They also cite anxiety about intermittent sexual function problems, conflict over fertility issues, uncertainty about whether or not to share fantasies or watch erotic videos, as well as discomfort with specific sexual scenarios and techniques. However, when exploring quality sex and satisfaction, these difficulties with function or behaviors don't tell the whole story.

HOW YOU THINK AND WHAT YOU DO

Traditionally, you focused on what you did in the bedroom and how you performed (e.g., erections, lubrication, intercourse, orgasm) to determine whether the sex was "great" and how satisfied you should feel. In truth, satisfaction is actually determined by how you *think* about sex—what you assume sex should be like, what you expect, and what you focus on. Use Exercise 3.1 to think about your honest learning. Because the meaning of sex is so important, our thoughts and expectations are crucial to sexual and relationship satisfaction.

• • • • • • •

EXERCISE 3.1 MY ASSUMPTIONS AND BELIEFS ABOUT SEX AND SATISFACTION

Take a moment to consider what you have learned to believe about sex. This is not an easy exercise, but it can help you appreciate and accept your honest sexuality. Reflect on the following five statements and write down your ideas or thoughts:

1. *I learned that sex is ...*
2. *The role that sex should play in my life and relationship is ...*
3. *When my partner and I share sex, we should ...*
4. *If my parents were watching us have sex, they would think ...*
5. *The key ingredients for satisfying sex are ...*

Realistic, age-appropriate, accurate sexual expectations are essential for genuine satisfaction. This is at the heart of GES. Of course, the actual sexual interaction is important, but great sex is not how wild or hard intercourse is but rather how you organize your thoughts (cognitions), especially your expectations, to assure sexual satisfaction. If great sex were as simple as technical performance, then professional athletes and Olympians would have the best sex and ordinary people would be sexually doomed. This, of course, is not the case. Rather, your cognitions—your beliefs, assumptions, standards, perceptions, attributions, and expectations—can either set up dissatisfaction and doom you to sexual misery or help build and ensure sexual desire, pleasure, and satisfaction.

It is crucial to be realistic and positive in order to ensure quality couple sex and sexual satisfaction. Exercise 3.2 will help you identify common mistakes in thinking that limit sexual pleasure and satisfaction, as well as show you a healthy, accurate way to think and cooperate with your partner. Clear thinking promotes sexual satisfaction. You need to "think smart."

> **Realistic, age-appropriate, accurate sexual expectations are essential for genuine satisfaction.**

Consider your typical ways of thinking during sex by taking the "Sexual Self-Talk Quiz" (Exercise 3.2).

• • • • • • •

EXERCISE 3.2 THE SEXUAL SELF-TALK QUIZ

Place a check in front of the statements that reflect your thoughts when sex does not go well.

1. _____ "I don't know what to do."
2. _____ "I enjoy the touching, and it allows us to feel close."
3. _____ "I am totally inadequate."
4. _____ "It is so nice to be together."
5. _____ "I should just give up. I always fail sexually."
6. _____ "Let's rest a while and try lovemaking again."
7. _____ "I'm not any good at this."
8. _____ "We don't have to be perfect. We accept each other and feel good about our relationship no matter what happens sexually."
9. _____ "I must resolve this problem or my partner will go to a different lover."
10. _____ "We just need some time to relax."
11. _____ "My partner must be angry with me."
12. _____ "Enjoying the pleasure of being close and touching is more important than sexual performance."
13. _____ "What's wrong with me? Sex is supposed to be automatic."
14. _____ "We've had a really long day with too much stress. How about a rain check?"
15. _____ "I should turn my partner on, get him/her sexually aroused. I want to but I'm not any good."
16. _____ "We always find a way to enjoy ourselves even when things don't work like in a movie."
17. _____ "My partner doesn't find me attractive anymore."
18. _____ "It is reassuring that we accept each other even when sex doesn't go well."

19. _____ *"Sex is a problem and our relationship is in trouble."*

20. _____ *"Sometimes our sex is great and sometimes it's poor. We do pretty well."*

Add the number of odd-numbered items you checked, then the number of even-numbered items. The odd-numbered items are negative, self-defeating thoughts that cause emotional distress. The even-numbered items are constructive, positive thoughts that inspire realistic sexual satisfaction. If your positive score is higher than your negative score, you are well positioned for GES. If not, you now are aware of the need to think reasonably and constructively about your sexual life.

SMART THINKING FUNDAMENTALS

The important factors in life (including sex) are not simple or one-dimensional, no matter how much we wish they were. In truth, there are elaborate elements involved in the human experience of quality couple sex. The idyllic societal notion of "Great Sex" is that it should always be ideal. This sets up an unrealistic expectation for the unlikely alignment of all the stars in the "Great Sex Constellation"—the simultaneous, flawless merging of the infinite variations in physical performance, stamina and efficiency, psychological excellence, and romantic mood. Great sex is distorted as the "dreaming on a star" wish to recreate the intensity of adolescent sex or the Hollywood-type sex portrayed in movies. With so many elements to blend perfectly, this version of great sex becomes the Sexual Power Ball Lottery. It may be fun to gamble, but you must realize that the odds are against you. Genuinely satisfied couples abandon the Great Sex Chase and adopt GES. Build your quality couple sexuality expectations on the GES perspective that is grounded on reality, balanced with scientific knowledge, built on genuine life experiences, and inspired with awareness, comfort, pleasure, and eroticism (Table 3.1).

Table 3.1 Smart Thinking: Core Principles of the GES Approach

- Sex plays a positive and durable role in your relationship and day-to-day existence through each stage of your life.
- Sexual satisfaction does not have a simple cause in spite of people's longing for simplicity. Satisfaction is complicated. It is multi-causal, multidimensional, and has multiple dynamics for you and your partner.
- Satisfaction with your sexual life is fundamentally grounded on realistic physical, psychological, and relationship expectations. Unrealistic expectations precipitate frustration, distress, and a sense of failure.
- The emphasis on perfect sex performance in our society is self-defeating and needs to be replaced by the GES model, which realistically recognizes the inherent variability of couple sex.
- Accept that there is no right or wrong way to be sexual. Respect, value, and integrate your individual and gender differences. Cooperate for sexual satisfaction.
- Achieving satisfaction in a relationship requires you to cooperate as an intimate team.
- GES recognizes that among satisfied couples, the quality of sex varies from day to day and from exceptional to good to mediocre or even dysfunctional.

THE COGNITIVE/BEHAVIORAL/EMOTIONAL (CBE) MODEL

Relationships and healthy sex have their own intricacies. They do not fit well into discrete, rigid categories; neither do they thrive in incomprehensible chaos. Psychological, relational, and sexual factors are interactive and complementary.

To illustrate the intricacy of your individual and relationship health, focus on your cognitive/behavioral/emotional psychological features. Your sexual growth goals include CBE dimensions (Figure 3.1). You and your partner have your own cognitions about yourself and your relationship, behavioral patterns, and unique personal and relational feelings.

Cognitions or Thoughts

Your thoughts about yourself and your relationship constitute the core factor in relational satisfaction and stability. Ideally, your marriage or serious relationship meets your needs for intimacy and security better than any other relationship. The essence of a

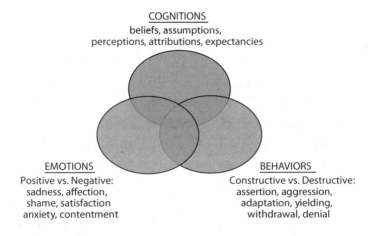

COGNITIONS
beliefs, assumptions,
perceptions, attributions, expectancies

EMOTIONS
Positive vs. Negative:
sadness, affection,
shame, satisfaction
anxiety, contentment

BEHAVIORS
Constructive vs. Destructive:
assertion, aggression,
adaptation, yielding,
withdrawal, denial

Figure 3.1 Your psychological dimensions: CBE model.

healthy relationship is a respectful, trusting commitment. Accept yourself with your personal strengths and vulnerabilities. Healthy cognitive awareness is not a "feel good" concept, but a genuine personal awareness and acceptance. Your partner respecting and loving you for who you really are, including vulnerabilities and "warts," is very personally validating.

Cognitively, trust has two components. The belief that your partner has your best interest in mind is the positive component. A healthy relationship is based on a positive influence process. Being in this relationship brings out something healthy in each of you. You believe in each other and hope for the best for yourselves as a couple. You have a "team" mentality.

The second component of trust is the belief that your partner would not do something intentionally to harm you or the relationship. That does not mean that you won't be disappointed or frustrated with your partner, but the crucial cognitive component is intentionality, trusting your partner does not have a negative agenda.

Commitment also has a crucial cognitive component. You make choices and value your choices. The commitment to your relationship is a cognitive choice to work together to share your lives and problem-solve difficult issues.

Behaviors or Actions

Behaviorally, the key element is that your individual and couple behaviors are congruent with and reinforce your cognitions. Important behavioral components are building a secure, stable couple bond; reinforcing your couple identity; implementing problem-solving skills so issues are resolved, modified, or accepted; and building intimacy skills. Emotional intimacy nurtures your bond, and sexual intimacy energizes your bond.

Emotions or Feelings

Emotions are crucial in relational and sexual satisfaction. Emotions are more complex than the "pop psych" adage of "just feel good." A key element in individual and couple well-being is that cognitions, behaviors, and emotions are congruent. Emotions both reflect cognitions and behaviors, as well as influence them. A key element in positive emotions is a sense of acceptance from your partner, who loves, respects, and accepts you for who you really are. Key to trusting your emotions is feeling that there is a secure attachment and that your partner "has your back."

A necessary element in emotional intimacy is to feel safe and connected, that you and your partner can share and process positive and negative emotions without fear of judgment or rejection. The key sexual emotions involve desire and satisfaction: you anticipate and feel deserving of sexual pleasure. Rather than demanding a perfect sex performance (Hollywood-type sex), you accept a variable, flexible couple sexuality that blends intimacy, pleasuring, and eroticism. Positive, realistic sexual expectations lead to sexual satisfaction. Couple sexuality is integrated into your real-life relationship so that it contributes 15 to 20% to relational vitality and satisfaction.

Your Relationship

The interpersonal dimension requires being emotionally connected with your partner and feeling like intimate, erotic friends. Extending the CBE dimensions to your relationship, your couple *identity* or "relationship personality" is your shared thoughts about who you are as a couple, how your relationship and sexuality should function, how you balance individual autonomy and relationship cohesion. Your interactions reflect your level of *cooperation*. The ability to address conflicts and problem-solve is crucial in a serious relationship and has significant implications for sexual desire and satisfaction. Feelings reflect your *emotional intimacy*. These relationship dimensions require you to blend your sexual desires with intimate teamwork, and find the right balance of intimacy and eroticism, which facilitates sexual desire and function.

Thoughts "Rule": The Five Kinds of Cognitions

When it comes to determining your sexual satisfaction, the psychological dimensions—how you think (cognitions), what you do (behaviors), and how you feel (emotions)—all contribute and make a difference. Your cognitions, however, are premier and lead the way. They facilitate your emotions—the feelings that tell you how satisfied you are with your sex life. Five kinds of cognitions (Epstein & Baucom, 2002) comprise what you think is great sex, and these support, or undermine, your sexual satisfaction. Appreciate that these cognitions are momentous and interactive: they flow one to the other.

1. Beliefs or *standards* about sex and our bodies develop from our family, friends, experiences growing up, and our community and culture. These include "sex should always be intimate" or "if love is real, sex should be perfect" or "masturbation is bad." From these beliefs you

2. make *assumptions* about sex, such as "sex is good" or "sex is dirty." These beliefs and assumptions influence

3. your *perceptions* or selective attention, what you notice or "filter" about your feelings and actions, and your partner and sex. If you learned, for example, that "sex is dirty," your filters will monitor lovemaking for signs of disinterest or disgust, so you misperceive the meaning of a frown

or your partner's seeming passivity. The combination of your beliefs, assumptions, and perceptual filters influence

4. the *attributions* (interpretations of cause and effect) you make, such as "Because sex is dirty (belief) and because he/she is frowning (perception), he/she must be disappointed or disgusted (attribution)." Or; "He/she doesn't initiate sex anymore so I am no longer sexy and he/she doesn't love me." These attributions subsequently influence your

5. *expectations,* what you anticipate, such as "Our sex life is going to get worse." This "self-fulfilling prophecy" reinforces your beliefs, assumptions and perceptions, and, in turn, influences your feelings and behaviors.

Table 3.2 illustrates your sexual thoughts and processes.

Appreciating these thought processes can be a powerful tool to enhance your sexual understanding. You can determine your own course to relationship and sexual satisfaction. Your cognitions or internal "self-talk" seems automatic and accurate, although in truth you are actively involved in shaping them and you are at risk of distortion and error. Understanding that cognitions are not facts offers you self-awareness, flexibility, and powerful tools for couple cooperation and increasing sexual satisfaction.

The following case illustrates a couple with a sexual problem, the type of relationship cognitions they experienced, and how they approached the change process. Understanding your own cognitions can help you correct harmful ideas that limit your satisfaction, and encourage constructive cognitions that promote cooperation as an intimate team.

BRANDON AND MELISSA

Brandon regularly had erectile dysfunction (ED) about which he held several self-defeating, unrealistic assumptions and beliefs: "I'm a failure." "I want to but I can't please Melissa." He believed

Table 3.2 Examples of Positive versus Negative Sexual Cognitions

Kind of Cognition	Description	Unreasonable, Negative Thoughts	Constructive, Positive Thoughts
Assumptions	What each believes sex and relationships actually are.	Happy couples have great sex all the time.	Sexual quality varies from one experience to another in a healthy relationship.
Beliefs or Standards	What each believes sex and relationships should be.	Sex should be perfect.	Sex can contribute a 15%–20% positive energy to our relationship.
Perceptions	What each notices about sexual behaviors.	Our sex is only physical and we don't talk or look into each other's eyes.	Our sex is passionate, lustful one time, personal and intimate another time.
Attributions	Causal and responsibility explanations for sexual experiences.	Our sex is not perfect/a romantic movie/a porn flick, which means we have a flawed relationship.	Our sex is regular, variable, and fits into our real life.
Expectancies	Predictions of what will occur during sex.	Our sex will get worse, and we will get divorced.	Our sex life is developing and growing. We can enjoy sexuality into our 60s, 70s, and 80s.

that "Melissa is upset with me; I don't know what to do. I have to avoid sex or I'll fail again" (expectancy). He puzzled, "What's wrong with me? Sex and erections are supposed to be automatic" (assumption). Such negative cognitions precipitated feelings of anxiety, inadequacy, self-blame, embarrassment, and hopelessness. In reaction, he fluctuated from avoidance and silence to irritation and blaming. He felt anxious and argued with Melissa if she made any sexual initiation.

Melissa thought, "He doesn't love me anymore!" (negative attribution). "I should always turn him on" (unreasonable assumption). "He's not aroused (perception), so I am a failure (attribution)." I should be responsive and aroused" (assumption). "He's quiet so he must be angry with me" (attribution). "I have to talk to him about it or it will get worse" (assumption and predictive expectancy). "I don't know what to do. He feels terrible, and it is my fault" (attribution). Such negative thinking precipitated feeling anxious, frustrated, inadequate, and lonely. Fueled by these feelings, Melissa attempted to engage the problem by questioning Brandon, "What's wrong?" which he attributed as blame, and reacted with counterblame: "It's your fault!" Stung by his words, she was avoidant and silent for several hours, after which she became critical: "No, it's your fault. There is something sexually wrong with you."

When you recognize that much of this tension and distress is caused by negative, unrealistic, and erroneous thinking, you can begin to change these patterns. You can replace alienating, catastrophic cognitions, emotions, and behaviors by developing accurate, constructive and cooperative cognitions and behaviors. Brandon would do better to adopt realistic, accurate thoughts about sex, such as "Sex is not automatic." "My body is not a machine." "Sex function problems are normal." "My body needs relaxation to function well so I'll ask for a non-demand massage." "We can find other ways to pleasure each other." "We're a team." "We'll discuss alternative sexual scenarios;" or "We can cooperate for mutual pleasure." "Sex is about sharing pleasure and eroticism."

Melissa can adopt constructive cognitions such as "He lost his erection. No problem. I'm his partner. I can help him to relax and we can try again or shift to an erotic, non-intercourse scenario." "I don't need to blame myself for his erection going down." "I enjoy stimulating him." "He must be distracted or worried." Or, "I want to accept him, and help him accept himself without having to perform all the time." Or, "I'll invite him to enjoy the pleasure of my touch to shift focus from performance to sensual pleasure."

Together they cooperate, express constructive notions such as "sexual problems are normal now and then. Let's use an erotic non-intercourse scenario." Or "Nothing important is wrong. Great sex varies and we are an intimate team. Should we take a rain check?"

Perhaps the most important cognitive strategy is the 85% guideline. This reminds you that typically sex transitions from comfort to pleasure to arousal to erotic flow to intercourse in 85% of encounters. When the sex does not flow, you can transition to an erotic, non-intercourse scenario or a cuddly, sensual scenario so you end the encounter in a positive way.

SATISFIED COUPLES HAVE REALISTIC SEXUAL "SCRIPTS"

Sexual satisfaction is about personal and relationship "meaning" more than bedroom gymnastics. In fact, even among couples who experience sexual dysfunctions—including low sex desire, erectile dysfunction, premature ejaculation, difficulty having orgasm, or pain during intercourse, many maintain sexual satisfaction. It is less the behavior (the sex function problem) and more the meaning and feelings that determine the quality of your sexual relationship and feelings of satisfaction.

For example, Laumann et al. (1994) reported that even among couples who experienced ongoing sexual dysfunctions, a good number were sexually satisfied. For example, among "very happy" couples, 21% reported lack of sex interest, 10% noted erectile dysfunction, 17% indicated poor lubrication, 14% revealed inhibited orgasm, 18% rapid orgasm, and 8% sexual pain (dyspareunia). While these couples reported multiple function limitations, they were "very happy," which indicates that sexual function is only part of the sexual satisfaction equation. It is the *meaning* of the function difficulty and how they accommodate themselves to it that carries the day.

Byers & Grenier (2004) studied couples where the man ejaculated prematurely and found that the negative impact was not determined by the rapid orgasm but rather by the significance (meaning) of this for him and especially for his partner. For couples where the man sometimes ejaculated quickly, the partners flexibly adapted so that the meaning was not negative, and satisfaction was not undermined. Byers and Grenier suggested that, "It may be that although partners are dissatisfied with the time of ejaculation, they have developed *sexual scripts* that allow them to experience sexual pleasure through other forms of stimulation" (p. 269). Sexual scripts is a label that captures the blend of thoughts (beliefs, assumptions, perceptions, attributions, and expectations) that encompass the meaning of the issue and the way in which to handle it. The GES approach encourages you to develop flexible "sexual scripts," including alternative erotic scenarios and techniques.

REALISTIC, CONSTRUCTIVE COGNITIONS

Healthy couples do not self-destruct when there is a sexual problem. Satisfaction does not rest on this one time. They have a repertoire of constructive, realistic sexual scripts (see Table 3.3) that help generate positive feelings (e.g., acceptance, comfort) and

Table 3.3 Examples of Realistic, Cooperative GES Self-Talk

1. "We don't have to be perfect; we're sexually 'good enough.'"
2. "We are sexually comfortable and accept each other as we are."
3. "Let's shift to an alternative sex scenario."
4. "We always find a way to enjoy ourselves even when things don't work like in a movie."
5. "We've had a really long day with too much stress. We can relax sexually."
6. "It's okay to not always get aroused."
7. "Let's take a rain check until tomorrow."
8. "We have a good time sexually. It doesn't have to be a big production for us to feel pleased and cohesive."
9. "Our relationship is strong, and sex plays a positive role."
10. "Overall, our sexual relationship is pretty good."
11. "We're a couple, not stars in a porn movie."
12. "Let's share pleasure and eroticism so each of us feels good."

encourage constructive behaviors (e.g., reassuring words, relaxing touch, erotic scenarios, a rain check). Satisfied couples take a long-view of their sexual relationship.

PROBLEMS ARE OPPORTUNITIES

The GES approach views a sex difficulty as an opportunity to solidify cooperation and enhance the quality of your intimate relationship. Few problems in life so clearly offer us the opportunity to cooperate as a team and to promote personal and relationship satisfaction. To value problems as opportunities requires adjusting expectations about genuine couple sex. Realistic sexual expectations are the platform for sexual satisfaction because they determine the meaning that distinguishes satisfaction from dissatisfaction. Your relationship and sexual satisfaction involve *emotions* (e.g., feeling "good," contented, excited, appreciated) that are fundamentally grounded in the *cognitive* dimension (e.g., thoughts such as, "We please each other no matter what.") and shape the *behavioral* dimension (e.g., partner cooperation, cuddling and fondling, sharing pleasure and eroticism, enjoyable intercourse).

SUMMARY

In our GES approach, your thoughts and expectations are crucial for high-quality couple sex. You and your partner must develop realistic, accurate, and positive cognitions to promote couple sexual satisfaction. Learn to understand and appreciate the multiple dimensions of GES: physical, psychological, and interpersonal. Think in a healthy manner, be attentive to the current situation, and promote cognitions that involve:

- Positive beliefs and standards about what sex is and can be for you
- Accurate assumptions about what is, and what is not, great sex

- Flexible perceptions and careful "filters"
- Positive attributions of what causes sexual problems or tension, and what promotes satisfaction
- Realistic, positive expectations

These are powerful tools that you can use to build high sexual satisfaction. GES partners embrace thoughts such as:

- Sexual satisfaction varies from one experience to the next.
- Achieving high-quality sex is a lifelong process.
- Sex difficulties are opportunities for increased cooperation and intimacy.
- Satisfied couples cooperate as an intimate team.
- Quality sex is flexible: you adapt to the inevitable variability and difficulties.
- Sex fits real life, and real-life should be brought into your bedroom.
- The best sex involves being intimate and erotic partners.
- Quality sex is cooperative relationship sex.

4

The Best Sex Is Relationship Sex

SEXUAL HEALTH AND RELATIONSHIP SATISFACTION

When you value sex as inherently relational, your intimate relationship becomes your solid foundation for sexual vitality. A marker of lifelong sexual satisfaction is your acceptance that, by its nature, sex is relational. This is difficult for young couples to accept, partly because of the pressures to be attractive and the overemphasis on performance—being a "hot lover." With increasing maturity and comfort, your cooperation level as an intimate team emerges and grows.

Appreciate that your sexual satisfaction is inevitably and firmly grounded in your relationship. Reciprocally, your relationship satisfaction is firmly grounded on your sexual satisfaction. Sexual satisfaction "makes its bed" in your relationship's emotions, at times warmed by cohesion, at other times made passionate by your unique sexual voice. Intimacy and eroticism are integrated into your long-term relationship. This is the environment for great sexual quality. In this chapter, we will detail twelve avenues for intimacy that form the context for sexual satisfaction. It also summarizes research insights that can guide you toward relationship satisfaction and integrate the relationship aspects of couple sexuality.

YOUR RELATIONSHIP AS AN INTIMATE TEAM

Sexual health and satisfaction are more likely to occur when you work together as a team to achieve intimacy, comfort, pleasure, stress reduction, passion, mutual self-esteem, and joy in and

> **Your partner is your "sexual friend," and your relationship constitutes your "intimate team."**

out of the bedroom (Johnson, 2008). The mainstay of sexuality is giving and receiving pleasure-oriented touching.

You bond as a couple. You need each other as intimate and erotic friends. This is even truer after age 40, but learning this in your 20s and 30s will prepare you to face sexual problems that may come with your growing older and the aging of your relationship.

A valuable tool for couples seeking realistic sexual satisfaction is to consider the many avenues for intimacy. Sex is only one of a dozen ways that allows couples to feel close and connected. When one kind of intimacy gets too much priority, it can create a one-dimensional, narrow path that exerts excessive pressure on you to meet only that dimension—which, paradoxically, subverts intimacy. For example, you experience this imbalance when your partner expects sex without investing in other dimensions of intimacy, or you rule out sex unless emotional intimacy is abundant. The integration of a number of dimensions of intimacy is a feature of a quality relationship.

TWELVE PATHS TO RELATIONSHIP INTIMACY

The *Relationship Intimacy Assessment* (RIA; Metz, 1997) distinguishes twelve facets of intimacy. To ensure that your sexual relationship is vibrant, you need to cultivate ample avenues for intimacy that provide a strong environment for spirited sex. While you have your preferred paths or avenues to closeness, one is not necessarily better than another. It is important that you feel your preferred ways are valued and satisfying. Sex is one of the avenues, and often a preferred one, to enhance intimacy.

Each partner should complete separately the *Relationship Intimacy Assessment* (Exercise 4.1) before discussing your rankings. Be sure to read the description of each kind of intimacy as some meanings are different than the popular notions.

• • • • • • •

EXERCISE 4.1 RELATIONSHIP INTIMACY ASSESSMENT (RIA)

First, rank each of the 12 facets of relationship intimacy according to its importance to you as a means of sharing intimacy. Rank the "Most Important" facet as 1 and continue rankings to the "Least Important" facet as 12. After ranking the facets, rate your current level of satisfaction with each facet from 1 to 10, with 10 representing "Very High Satisfaction" and 1 representing "Very Low Satisfaction." Consider your preferences and current level of satisfaction.

When you and your partner have completed the RIA, share with openness. Then together rate your mutual desired level of satisfaction.

		Satisfaction	
Facet of Relationship Intimacy	Rank Order	Current Level	Desired Level
Recreation intimacy: sharing experiences of fun, leisure, sports, hobbies, recreation; finding ways of refilling your well of energy	____	____	____
Intellectual intimacy: sharing the world of ideas; a genuine interchange based on mutual respect for each other's intellectual capacities (reading, discussing)	____	____	____
Work intimacy: sharing common tasks, supporting each other in bearing responsibilities (e.g., raising children, house and yard chores)	____	____	____

(Continued)

(*Continued*)

Facet of Relationship Intimacy	Satisfaction		
	Rank Order	Current Level	Desired Level
Commitment intimacy: togetherness derived from dedication to a common cause or value (e.g., working for a political cause or social action)	———	———	———
Aesthetic intimacy: sharing experiences of beauty—music, nature, art, theater, dance, movies, poetry; drinking from the cup of beauty	———	———	———
Communication intimacy: being honest, trusting, truthful, loving; giving constructive, caring feedback; positive confrontation	———	———	———
Emotional intimacy: depth awareness and sharing of significant meanings and feelings; touching your innermost selves	———	———	———
Creative intimacy: helping each other to grow, being co-creators (not "reformers") of each other	———	———	———
Sexual intimacy sensual and emotional satisfaction; the experience of sharing eroticism and self-abandon in the physical merging of two persons; fantasies and desires	———	———	———
Crisis intimacy: standing together in the major and minor tragedies of life; closeness in coping with problems and pain	———	———	———
Conflict intimacy: standing up with and to each other; facing and struggling with differences; pursuing mutual conflict resolution	———	———	———
Spiritual intimacy: the "we-ness" of sharing ultimate concerns, the meanings of life, philosophies, religious experience	———	———	———

Source: Adapted from Clinebell & Clinebell (1970).

Often, partners have similar preferences and rankings. Are the top one-third of your ranked avenues to intimacy similar to your partner's rankings? How similar or different are your ratings of satisfaction? Do not judge your ratings; rather, discuss and be open to learn so you identify similarities, differences, and areas you can better appreciate as an opportunity to work toward common ground. Each partner has her or his priorities for feeling close, but all avenues play a positive role. This awareness of what makes you similar and different helps you appreciate the variety of ways you maintain and strengthen your intimate bond.

PRINCIPLES FOR STRONG RELATIONSHIP SATISFACTION

A careful review of the hundreds of studies investigating both why couples divorce and, more important, how couples succeed yields several qualities that characterize healthy couples.

> Among satisfied couples, feelings are more important and valued than being "right" or "fair."

Highly satisfied couples place a priority on their relationship—putting it before careers, kids, relatives, leisure activities (Table 4.1). Although in real life other priorities may draw more attention for a while, you know he or she is the number one priority to you. This is the foundation of feeling "special." When you know you are the top priority for your partner, you are free to dedicate yourself to other priorities. A balanced focus does not create resentment in your partner. When you know you have your partner's unconditional support, you seldom require it. Partner accessibility promotes openness and facilitates a "user-friendly" relationship.

An indispensable principle of contemporary satisfying relationships is that partners are "equals" and operate as a "team." While

Table 4.1 Principles of Relationship Satisfaction

- The relationship is your overall priority.
- Healthy relationships are established on personal equity.
- Cooperation is a priority.
- Each partner makes the other's satisfaction a main concern.
- Mutual emotional and sexual empathy are vital.
- Partners distinguish their feelings from behaviors.
- Conflict resolution has as its goal mutual emotional satisfaction.
- Relationship satisfaction is directly influenced by the quality of relationship conflict resolution.

gender roles may influence some role or task allocations, each person is of equal value and worth in the relationship. Because total equality in a relationship is neither possible nor desirable (e.g., exact split in childcare tasks, home maintenance, care of aging relatives), the standard for healthy couples is emotional "equity" or "relative fairness."

Satisfied couples cooperate, not compete. Partners may compete in sports or recreation, but otherwise they cooperate to establish mutual empathy (feelings) and mutual conflict resolution (behavior). They do not permit a winner-loser feeling. Couples who do well understand that life and relationships are not "fair."

You work toward making each partner feel respected and content rather than always having to make the "right" decision or develop the "perfect" action plan. Your partner's feelings are more important than "fairness" or the "right" decision. This is crucial because resentment is created when you put your partner first and this consideration is not reciprocated. When both put the other partner's feelings and happiness first, interact from the principle of "give to get," and seek emotional satisfaction in mutual problem solving, the emotional benefits can be wonderful.

This means that satisfied couples put a priority on mutual emotional and sexual empathy. Emotional empathy (acceptance, affirmation, comforting), combined with sexual pleasure, forms the "glue" of intimacy. You look to your committed relationship to give and receive emotional well-being.

FEATURES OF RELATIONSHIP SEXUALITY

When sex therapy developed as a professional field in the 1970s, the emphasis was on individual sex dysfunction, even though the treatment model focused on couple sex therapy. We now realize that sex is primarily an interpersonal team process; like any other team process, you win or lose as a team. This is not to negate that each partner is responsible for her/his desire, arousal, and orgasm, or that the same sexual encounter is often motivated and experienced in a different manner. Ultimately, the motivation for couple sexuality is to energize your bond and reinforce feelings of desire and desirability.

Generous Giving and Receiving of Pleasure

A crucial point of GES is generosity in giving and receiving pleasure-oriented touching. Sex is truly a team sport and the ultimate measure of satisfaction is not orgasm but, rather, feeling energized and bonded as a couple. You need each other as intimate and erotic friends.

Attending to your couple identity, cooperation, and intimate communication is a core component of maintaining vitality and satisfaction. Sexually, this means accepting that intimate, interactive, variable, flexible couple sexuality is more satisfying than perfect intercourse performance. Relationally, this means valuing a respectful, trusting, intimate relationship. Emotionally, feeling you have a secure bond is crucial. Trusting that your partner "has your back" is very reassuring.

Emotional and Sexual Balance

In satisfying relationships, your partner is more than just a sexual friend; he/she is your intimate friend. Unfortunately, seriously involved couples, whether married or not, too often become so preoccupied with managing day-to-day tasks involving jobs, parenting, household duties, community events, and life responsibilities that they treat their relationship (including sexuality) with benign neglect. Even though their relationship remains stable, they lose their spark and emotional intimacy. A healthy couple relationship promotes a vital sexual relationship that balances closeness and eroticism.

Closeness Is Not Enough   Traditionally, both professionals and the public believed that if the couple focused on increasing loving feelings and communication that the sex would be easy and take care of itself. This is not just a simplistic myth, it is also a dangerous one that can subvert quality couple sexuality. A healthy relationship involves both emotional intimacy and sexual intimacy (Perel, 2006). They are truly different, although ideally complementary, dimensions. Closeness is of central value in establishing couple identity, communication, and feeling connected. However, it may not improve sexual desire and function. A real danger is that some couples feel so close and intimate that it actually smothers sexual desire: they de-eroticize each other. They are such good, intimate friends that there is no space for sexual playfulness or eroticism.

In dating couples, the other extreme is even more common: a chaotic, tumultuous relationship that is highly sexually charged. There is romantic love and passionate sex, as well as anger, drama, and mistreatment. The point is that intimacy (characterized by closeness, safety, solid connection, empathy, cooperation) is a different dimension than eroticism (characterized by emotional intensity and sexual passion, risk-taking, creativity, mystery, unpredictability). In a healthy relationship, intimacy and eroticism are integrated into your couple sexual style.

Being Both an Intimate Friend and an Erotic Friend   The role of emotional intimacy is to nurture your bond. The role of sexual intimacy is to energize your bond, specifically to enhance feelings of desire and desirability. Sexuality can contribute 15% to 20% to relationship satisfaction when you see each other as intimate and erotic partners. It acts as a special relationship resource that helps maintain vitality and satisfaction. Quality couple sex cannot compensate for a deficit in respect, trust, or commitment—no matter what you see on TV shows or in the movies, or what you read online or hear on relationship talk shows. However, it plays a positive, integral role in energizing your relationship and contributing to relationship security, stability, vitality, and satisfaction. Sexuality serves a number of positive relational functions—a shared pleasure, a means to reinforce intimacy, a tension reducer, a way to strengthen self-esteem and feelings of attractiveness, as well as the traditional biological function of conceiving a planned, wanted child.

Multiple Roles and Meanings of Relationship Sex

It is important to realize that sex can have a number of roles and meanings throughout your relationship. In addition, it can have different roles for each partner, including changes in roles and meanings during a single sexual encounter. Sexuality can be a means to affirm love, a port in the storm during difficult times, a way of reenergizing after a conflict with a child, a way to reconnect after a period of physical or emotional distance. It can take the form of excitement and hope when trying to conceive a baby, a celebration after receiving a promotion, a way to recover from disappointment about not getting a house you bid on, a form of spiritual comfort after the death of your best friend.

The fact that sex can play a different role for one partner than the other is both natural and normal. This is an example of the variability and flexibility of healthy couple sexuality. For example, for one partner, a given sexual encounter might involve primarily a need for orgasm as a tension reducer, while for the other partner it may be a shared pleasure, a pleasant interlude in a hectic life. One partner might experience sex as close and warm; for the other, sex may serve the purpose of conceiving a child. Sex for one partner might be easy and nurturing, and for the other a way to reach out for validation of desirability and attractiveness. Of course, there are many encounters when the partners share a common meaning—when a sexual interlude becomes a way to reinforce and deepen intimacy, to share pleasure, or to engage in a playful encounter. Couples who incorporate the multiple roles and meanings of sexuality have a variable, flexible, resilient couple sexual style that can be well-integrated into their daily lives.

ROBERTO AND JILL

Roberto was a divorced 32-year-old man in a 4-year relationship with 33-year-old Jill, who had never been married. She had an 11-year-old son from a previous relationship and a 1-year-old son with Roberto. They were a serious couple but were hesitant to marry for a number of emotional and practical reasons. Roberto felt unfairly treated in his divorce. Few of Jill's friends were married, not because they didn't value marriage but because the reality of a marriage commitment felt too daunting. A major factor was that neither Roberto nor Jill had contemporary models of a satisfying, stable marriage.

In terms of couple identity, they were very involved with their 1-year-old and were cooperative parents. They were a lower middle class couple; both worked and contributed to joint expenses, including rent and food. In most ways they were a respectful couple, but not overly trusting, especially in terms of long-term plans and commitments. They were a sexually functional couple but were caught in the traditional power struggle of intercourse frequency.

Couple's lives are not organized around sex issues, nor should they be. The stimulus that caused Roberto and Jill to rethink their relationship was Roberto's opportunity to enter a 3-year management training program that could offer him a middle-class profession with an increased, stable income. However, it would entail being gone from the home for intensive training. Although he engaged in braggadocio, Roberto lacked confidence in his ability to learn, especially because of his reading skills. Would Jill be supportive of this training program? In fact, Jill was his biggest cheerleader. She urged him to pursue the program and offered to tutor him in reading.

Emotionally and practically, a relationship is a positive-influence process and brings out healthy parts of each person. This transition for Roberto and Jill required planning, coordination, and communication, particularly regarding child-care logistics. Roberto was at home less but he was much more helpful and engaged when he was there, rather than watching TV and drinking beer. Jill's respect for Roberto increased, and his ambition was as an excellent model for her older son.

Roberto asked Jill to celebrate his successful first year of training after he had passed the probationary period. Jill wanted to do something special, including sexually. She got a babysitter for their son and arranged for the older boy to spend a weekend with a friend's family. Roberto and Jill went to a hotel on the water that had a special weekend rate. Being away as a couple without children is a good opportunity to be sexual. Sex between Roberto and Jill on Friday night was functional, but not special. Sitting on the balcony looking out over the water on Saturday morning gave Jill the emotional courage to say she thought they could be a more intimate, more sexually fun couple. Would Roberto hear this as an invitation rather than a complaint or demand? His management training included problem-solving skills, and some of those listening and conflict-resolution skills were applicable to their relationship.

Roberto and Jill were stuck in the "intercourse-or-nothing" assumption. Jill had read about the five dimensions (gears) of touching (see Chapter 9) and the accompanying psychosexual skill exercises (McCarthy & McCarthy, 2009). She was particularly intrigued with the third (playful touch) and fourth (erotic, non-intercourse touch) kinds of touch. She suggested to Roberto that Saturday be a non-intercourse day. This afternoon she was willing to initiate an erotic date and asked whether he would be willing to initiate a playful date that evening. Roberto felt both surprised and pleased with Jill's creativity, experiencing a jolt of anticipation and desire he had not felt in months.

Jill's initiation was elaborate. She put on their favorite CD, bought a fragrant candle and body lotion, and focused on sensual self-entrancement arousal style (see Chapter 10); previously they'd always enjoyed mutual, partner-interaction arousal style with a quick switch to intercourse. This was the most sensual, pleasurable, erotic experience ever for Roberto. He felt she really enjoyed pleasuring him to orgasm rather than mechanically "doing him." Although she had planned to wait for the evening, Roberto was very enthusiastic about manually pleasuring Jill to orgasm, something he had never tried. He was quite surprised by the intensity of her erotic flow and orgasmic response. They took a nap, had a late lunch, and walked by the water. Walking and talking is a good milieu in which to share perceptions and feelings. Jill shared with Roberto that it was much easier for her to be orgasmic with manual and rubbing stimulation. Even though she enjoyed intercourse and could be orgasmic during intercourse, erotic stimulation to orgasm was her preference. This was news to Roberto, but the relationship had grown in the past few months and he was now open to being her intimate, erotic friend.

Roberto's evening initiation was less elaborate, but a lot of fun. While they showered (he hated baths), they enjoyed non-genital and genital touching. They dried each other off and, still nude, Roberto engaged Jill in salsa dancing. This evolved from playful to erotic to orgasm, using partner-interaction stimulation—with a focus on rubbing stimulation for Jill and oral stimulation for Roberto.

Over brunch and a walk on Sunday morning, they had two conversations. One was based on their desire to incorporate these new learnings and feelings into sex in their home. Intercourse would still be the main course, but not the only one. Sometimes they could have sexual fun and not need intercourse. The second conversation was the more important one. Couples do not realize that a major function of sex is to energize them to deal with important relationship issues. Roberto and Jill wanted to build a stronger, more resilient, more intimate bond based on respect and trust. They agreed to explore in the next few weeks and months whether they would value a marital commitment.

SUMMARY

The essence of a serious or marital relationship is a respectful, trusting commitment. Sex is not the core of your relationship, but it does contribute to energizing your bond and increasing feelings of desire and desirability. It isn't sex versus the relationship; these are complementary dimensions. Couple identity, cooperation, and emotional intimacy are vital components of a healthy relationship. Sexuality is complementary to those core components, not in opposition to them.

The trap to avoid is the traditional male-female conflict in which men value eroticism and women value intimacy. *Healthy couples value both intimacy and eroticism.* The man can be an intimate partner, and the woman can value her erotic voice and influence. This integration is the heart of deeply satisfying and meaningful couple sexuality. The challenge for couple sexual desire and satisfaction is to value your partnership's unique integration of intimacy and eroticism. Be sure to promote those features that support your relationship cohesion, and ensure that your sexual vitality energizes your relationship. These are essential for your couple satisfaction.

5

Creating Your Couple Sexual Style

Most couples begin their relationship with idealized romantic love and passionate sex. This is a very important phase because it gives you and your partner the courage to take the emotional risk and become involved in a serious relationship. However, by its nature this is a fragile, short-lived phase, usually lasting 6 months to a year, seldom more than 2 years (Fisher, 2004). The challenge for serious couples, married or unmarried, is to integrate intimacy and eroticism, hallmarks of a long-term relationship.

Pursuing the many facets of couple intimacy and working cooperatively as a team to resolve your normal conflicts prepares you to make a fundamental emotional choice about your couple sexual style. Traditionally, people believed that there was one couple sexual style that was best—the more intimacy and communication, the better the sex. However, it is now clear that "one size does not fit all," especially sexually. Couples need to establish a mutually comfortable level of intimacy that facilitates sexual desire and eroticism.

The McCarthys devoted an entire book to the topic of developing the right couple sexual style for every relationship (McCarthy & McCarthy, 2009). The two issues in your couple sexual style are integrating intimacy and eroticism with the right balance of personal *autonomy*—your "sexual voice"—and your *connection* as an "intimate team."

The four couple sexual styles (in order of frequency) are:

- Complementary—mine and ours
- Traditional—conflict minimizing
- Soul Mate—best friend
- Emotionally Expressive—fun and erotic

The key is to find a mutually comfortable, functional balance of each person's sexual voice and to connect as an intimate team whose integration of intimacy and eroticism facilitates sexual desire and satisfaction (Perel, 2006). Each couple sexual style has its strengths and, conversely, each has vulnerabilities. The challenge is to play to the strengths of your couple sexual style and to be aware of and monitor its vulnerabilities so you do not fall into traps that subvert healthy couple sexuality.

Each couple develops a unique expression of sexuality, which is neither static nor totally predictable. You forge a sexual style based on individual needs and preferences, with equal weight placed on your partner's needs and preferences so that you truly function as an intimate team.

Developing your unique couple sexual style will enhance desire, pleasure, and satisfaction.

> **The two issues in your couple sexual style are integrating intimacy and eroticism, and balancing personal *autonomy*— your "sexual voice"— and *connection* as an "intimate team."**

THE ELEMENTS OF A COUPLE SEXUAL STYLE

Intimacy

The first element in your couple style is intimacy. Intimacy allows you to feel safe and connected. Intimacy usually involves affectionate touch, and often sensual and playful touch. Empathy for your partner's feelings and sharing a range of emotions and experiences are core qualities of intimacy. Special feelings and experiences of intimacy include fond recollections of a walk in the woods or on the beach sharing your hopes, fears, and dreams; lying together in bed on a Saturday morning talking and touching; trusting that you can tell your partner about your project being rejected, knowing he or she will still love and respect you; receiving a big hug and passionate kiss when you return from a grueling trip; feeling that your partner is "there for you" as you deal with a health problem. Intimacy allows you to have faith that your partner understands and cares for *you* and is vitally interested in how you feel, how you think, what you do.

Eroticism

The second component of your couple sexual style is eroticism. It is a basic human need for both women and men to desire an energy charge that involves high levels (emotional and physical) of erotic flow and orgasm. Sexual pleasure and eroticism (whether enjoying erotic fantasies, focusing on genital stimulation, or having intercourse and orgasm) is a healthy dimension of your sexual self. Eroticism involves the freedom to let go, get lost and bask in pleasure, lose your self in passion and sexual abandonment. Eroticism includes manual, oral, and rubbing touch, as well as intercourse.

The challenge for quality couple sexuality is to integrate intimacy and eroticism. Some women, for example, enjoy intimacy and pleasuring but feel inhibited with passionate erotic expression, wrongly believing this is the man's domain. On the other hand, some partners believe their role is to be sexually dramatic and wild all the time. Some men feel that valuing intimacy and non-demand pleasuring is weak and makes them appear less macho and sexual (especially in the eyes of other males). This is cultural nonsense and subverts healthy female, male, and couple sexuality. In truth, both men and women are healthier and more satisfied when they affirm intimacy, pleasure, and eroticism in their relationship.

Strengths of Each Couple Sexual Style

Individual and couple growth goals are highly influenced by your couple sexual style. Let's first examine each sexual style and highlight its strengths.

Complementary Couple Sexual Style   The most commonly chosen couple sexual style emphasizes that each partner has his or her own voice, including developing "his," "hers," and "our" bridges to sexual desire, including preferred erotic scenarios and techniques. Each partner values intimacy and eroticism and is able to feel and express integrated sexuality in their relationship. You accept and validate your partner's sexual feelings and preferences, realizing you are not clones of each other. This is the most common style, in part because each partner affirms sexual autonomy and reinforces the crucial importance of being an intimate, erotic team.

Traditional Couple Sexual Style   This is the most stable relationship style and the least emotionally volatile. Your approach to intimacy and sexuality is based on traditional gender roles. The man initiates sex, with the focus on frequency and intercourse. The woman initiates affection, with the focus on emotional intimacy. There are clear roles, and conflict is minimized. For the man, the emphasis is on intercourse, and sex is his domain. The woman's domain is emotions, especially communication and closeness, and she downplays her sexual voice and eroticism. With clarity about roles and meanings, sex requires little negotiation or intense emotion, much less drama.

A strength of this couple style is that you have the support of family, friends, and community. There are a number of people and institutions supportive of your bond. Sex is not a prime factor; sex is a means of procreation, and your lives center on parenting and family. A paradox is that this is the couple sexual style that can most easily accept having a nonsexual marriage, especially if you continue affectionate touch. You are very unlikely to break up because of sexual dysfunction or sex problems.

Soul Mate Couple Sexual Style   This is the "ideal" couple style in our society. The assumption is that more intimacy and communication mean better sex. You value the closeness and mutuality of your relationship. You focus on partner interaction arousal and mutuality more than any other couple style. You celebrate a secure bond based on intimacy. Sharing high levels of intimacy and eroticism with the same person is highly validating. The sense of trust and acceptance is powerful, both individually and as a couple. This couple style is highly valued by our culture; other couples are supportive and, in fact, envy you.

Emotionally Expressive Couple Sexual Style   This is the fun and passionate style. You put the highest priority on eroticism and expression of strong emotions. This is the stuff of R-rated movies, love songs, and *Cosmo*. You are the most resilient sexually and emphasize sex as high energy, fun, exploring, and experimental. You see each other as the "wild thing." You test the limits, use porn videos, play out role enactment scenarios, and when hurt or angry you cry, yell, and are sexual. There is a lot of emotional and sexual passion, and other couples envy your energy and sexual vitality.

Your Couple Sexual Style: Avoiding Traps and Ensuring Growth

Each sexual style has its vulnerabilities and traps. You want to be aware of and monitor them so they don't subvert healthy sexuality, and your sexual style remains vital and satisfying.

Complementary Couple Sexual Style   The major trap for the complementary couple is treating your sexual relationship with "benign neglect." You've established a healthy, satisfying couple sexual style and mistakenly believe you can just go on automatic pilot. Tempting, but self-defeating. Couple sexuality cannot rest on its laurels; it needs new inputs and energy.

You need to devote time and energy to your sexual relationship at every stage, whether you've been together 5, 20, or 40 years. You can blend sex techniques, both small and major. A worthwhile growth strategy is to introduce every 6 months a new intimacy, pleasuring, or erotic technique. In the next 6 months, it is your partner's turn. Thus, each year, two new sexual techniques would be added to keep your couple style vital and satisfying. These could be relatively minor changes: try a different lotion for a sexual massage, a different intercourse position or thrusting motion, have sex in the guest bedroom or family room, be sexual in the morning or early evening.

Major sexual changes could include going away for a weekend without children for the first time in years, introducing a one-way erotic scenario, experimenting with two self-entrancement sexual scenarios, or introducing a vibrator into couple sex. The goal is not to prove something to yourself or your partner, but to add freshness and variety that enhances your chosen couple sexual style.

A second major vulnerability inherent in the complementary couple style is a change in your lifestyle, especially becoming parents. A strength of this style is a sense of emotional, practical, and sexual equity. With the introduction of children, the trap is a diminishment of your couple relationship, especially sexually. A common pattern is that sexual satisfaction goes down at the birth of a first child, and does not rebound until the last child leaves home. In confronting this trap, you acknowledge that the most important bond in a family is the husband-wife bond. The role of intimacy and sexuality is to energize your bond and reinforce feelings of desire and desirability. The specific suggestion is to set aside quality couple time, including going away overnight or for a weekend without your children. Intimacy and sexuality are an integral part of couple time. Be committed to maintaining healthy couple sexuality through the parenting years. You can be both a parental team and a sexual team.

Complementary Style Case Illustration: Joe and Mary When Joe and Mary were married 12 years ago, they expected to be a traditional sexual couple. Two years into their marriage, Mary began lobbying for greater sexual parity. She wanted Joe to realize that she had her own sexual feelings and preferences. Her "sexual voice" was different than his, but not second class. Joe enjoyed "quickies," which were fine with Mary as long as they were balanced by intimate, interactive sexual scenarios that included 20 minutes of pleasuring and transitioned to intercourse at high levels of erotic flow.

Joe found Mary's emphasis on variable, flexible sexual scenarios and techniques very inviting. He said, "Most men settle for 'meat-and-potatoes sex.' I'm lucky to be married to a partner who appreciates everything from a quickie intercourse to a gourmet sexual experience." Joe came to value Mary's focus on warm, sharing afterplay. It took him longer to learn to value sensual/playful encounters that did not transition to intercourse, but ultimately he realized they also had a positive role.

A very important experience in learning to value their complementary couple sexual style was when Joe was laid off from work. This was totally unexpected, and negatively impacted his self-esteem. At first, Joe would push intercourse frequency to compensate for feelings of rejection. Then he'd go to the other extreme of sexual avoidance to hide his embarrassment at not providing an income. Rather than taking this personally and overreacting, Mary took the initiative and suggested comforting touch when Joe was feeling low and sexual touch as a way to energize them. Sexual touch served as a "port in the storm" during Joe's 15 weeks of unemployment. This was a way of being emotional and sexual allies during a stressful time.

Joe and Mary valued their chosen couple sexual style because it fit their real life. They loved and respected each other, while realizing they were not clones of each other. Mary appreciated Joe's emphasis on maintaining a regular rhythm of sexual connection, and Joe enjoyed Mary's emphasis on the varied roles and meanings of intimacy, touch, and sexuality.

Traditional Couple Sexual Style Couples who adopt this sexual style value traditional gender roles. Thus, it is not surprising that gender vulnerabilities appear as the man ages. These age-related vulnerabilities can begin in the 40s but certainly in the 50s. The man is no longer able to function autonomously, and needs partner involvement and genital stimulation. In other words, the woman is invited to take a more active role in the pleasuring/eroticism process, particularly penile stimulation to enhance erotic flow. The woman, especially during and after menopause, needs partner acceptance and support for sexual arousal. Your sexual relationship becomes increasingly interactive as you need each other more. The traditional trap for the man is to feel that his partner's emotional stress and sensual needs are rejecting his sexuality. The traditional trap for the woman involves feeling that her intimacy needs are not validated, that sex is about his erotic needs. To address this and to enhance couple sexuality, a valuable strategy is for the man, on occasion, to initiate an intimacy date that does not lead to intercourse. The partners share intimacy and sensuality as valuable in itself. An enhancement strategy is for the woman to initiate and play out her own erotic scenario, whether once a month or every 6 months. You can respect traditional gender roles while adding positive elements to your chosen couple sexual style.

Traditional Style Case Illustration: Sarah and William   Sarah and William very much valued their traditional couple sexual style. They were active members of a Lutheran congregation, and their three children were involved in church youth activities. Sarah had been raised Methodist, but gladly converted when they married. Both William and Sarah valued the stability of their marriage and the clarity of their gender and sexual roles. William placed high value on their mutual commitment to monogamy, and Sarah felt secure and fulfilled in both the mother and wife roles.

William lost his erection during intercourse for the first time at age 41. Rather than allowing this to result in emotional drama, without saying anything, they just held each other. Two days later when William initiated sex, Sarah was very responsive, stimulated

William, and guided him into her when he was highly aroused. Without focusing on sexual function, William and Sarah transitioned to a more interactive sexual style.

Especially after struggles with children and taking care of her father-in-law after his stroke, Sarah turned to William for comforting touch. Although at times this transitioned to intercourse, usually they used touch for connection and support. Unlike the offspring of other couples they knew, their children did not act out. They adopted their parents' pattern of staying focused on real-life academic and developmental issues, not becoming destabilized by sexual risk taking. Maritally, sexually, and in terms of family, Sarah and William felt their chosen couple sexual style fit them well. They were committed to not falling into the traps of the traditional couple sexual style.

Soul Mate Couple Sexual Style   There are two major vulnerabilities in what previously had been viewed as the "ideal" sexual style. The first is that there is so much closeness in the soul mate style that the couple de-eroticizes each other. That is why so many couples now choose the complementary couple sexual style, which allows each partner to retain his/her sexual voice. In order to address the danger of de-eroticizing, each partner can initiate a playful sexual scenario. Your secure bond can be "spiced-up" by sexual playfulness. Your partner is a sexual person with whom you can play, including using "sex toys." In addition, many couples use nicknames for her breasts, penis, vagina, testicles, and other body parts.

The second major vulnerability of this style is that the requirement for mutual desire and response can reduce sexual frequency. Awareness of your partner's feelings and receptivity to sex is a strength, but the rigid requirement of sexual equality can stifle sex initiation. The antidote is to initiate a "selfish" sexual scenario, whether once a month or every 6 months. This establishes a different sexual dimension that can promote "space" in your soul mate style. Examples include initiating in your idiosyncratic way, playing out a scenario that is particularly erotic for you, acting out a one-way erotic scenario in which you are the receiving partner, or using a role-enactment arousal scenario such as being blind-folded or lightly tied with crepe paper or restrained with hand cuffs while your partner gets to "do you." Remember, good sex is variable. Demanding mutual desire, arousal, and orgasm at each encounter is self-defeating for any couple sexual style.

Soul Mate Style Case Illustration: Karen and Jess   Karen and Jess reveled in their soul mate couple sexual style. This was Karen's sec-ond marriage and Jess's first, and they were committed to main-taining a satisfying and stable marriage. Having a special bond that focused on emotional and sexual intimacy was a shared value.

Karen's siblings and friends kidded her about how much time and energy she put into Jess and the marriage. For Karen, intimacy was worth the time and effort. They talked and touched on a daily basis, and emphasized mutuality in all realms, including sexual-ity. Jess felt that sharing emotions and touch was more important than intercourse and orgasm. He'd married at age 36 after much dating and two cohabitating relationships. Jess told Karen he no longer had a need for "party sex." He wanted an intimate, closely bonded relationship. Karen agreed with Jess; both her first mar-riage and subsequent relationships involved sexual intensity that was ultimately destabilizing.

Jess and Karen were aware of the trap of de-eroticizing the spouse, and wanted to be sure that this not happen to them. They wanted sexuality to play an energizing role in their marriage, so they agreed that each month one partner would initiate an erotic play date, which could involve mutual or one-way pleasur-ing. Over the months, Jess found that he really enjoyed playing out erotic scenarios with Karen. It was a very special energiz-ing experience. On her part, Karen found that "selfish sex" was highly empowering. These sexual experiences broke the "tyranny of mutuality." Karen and Jess maintained their soul mate couple sexual style while allowing playfulness and eroticism to spice up their couple sexuality.

Emotionally Expressive Couple Sexual Style The emotionally expressive couple has quite different vulnerabilities than those with other sexual styles. Desire is robust and resilient. The problem is that you wear each other out with the level and frequency of emotional and sexual intensity. In addition, when hurt or angry, you're inclined to say or do something that breaks a crucial personal or sexual boundary. The worst example is saying ugly, destructive things while lying in bed nude after a negative sexual experience. These include, "If I knew you were so frigid, I would never have married you." Or "If you can't get it up, why do you bother to stay alive." Such remarks can cause irreparable damage.

A crucial agreement for emotionally expressive couples is to forbid "nuclear bomb" statements. You never impulsively "drop the bomb," no matter how angry, hurt, or drunk you are. Being clear with yourself and your partner about the damage to you and the relationship makes it highly unlikely that either of you will cross that boundary.

Emotionally Expressive Style Case Illustration: Lisa and Ryan Lisa and Ryan loved their relationship and the vital, robust sex that was an integral part of it. Two years ago, friends from a local pub voted Ryan and Lisa the "sexiest couple in the neighborhood."

Thirty-three year old Lisa was a business consultant—a "road warrior" who traveled three or four days a week. Many times Ryan, an accountant, would meet her for the weekend if she was working in an interesting city or part of the country. Their weekend sex was erotic, fun, and varied. They put the "sex" channel on in the hotel room and used the X-rated movie as a bridge to sexual desire. Lisa and Ryan prided themselves on being sexually adventurous, whether acting out erotic scenarios (Ryan especially was aroused by domination-submission scenarios) or using sex toys (Lisa enjoyed using rings and balls). Desire and eroticism was their forte.

They made fun of traditional couples who were tied to "vanilla sex." Lisa and Ryan agreed to a nontraditional approach to monogamy. Each could engage in a "sexual friendship" or "recreational sex" as long as there was no serious emotional connection and it did not involve someone the partner knew. They felt that having an alternative sexual outlet would energize their couple sex. Rebonding their relationship provided a special erotic charge.

Lisa and Ryan were cognizant of the traps of too much drama and using "nuclear bomb" statements. They did engage in spirited arguments and used sex as a way to reconnect rather than bearing a grudge. Particularly important to Lisa was that Ryan did not use as a weapon against her the fact that she had been fired for unethical conduct early in her career. Likewise, Lisa was sensitive to the most painful emotional experience in Ryan's life—his brother's suicide.

Lisa and Ryan genuinely played to the strengths of their chosen couple sexual style, savoring the fun and eroticism.

Play to Your Strengths

A recurring theme in healthy partnerships is to play to the strengths of your chosen style and be aware of "traps" so you do not subvert your intimate relationship. Growth goals emphasize the strengths of your chosen couple style. However, it is just as important to be aware of the traps/vulnerabilities and address these in a preventative manner. If an issue becomes problematic, address it in the acute phase where it can be resolved more easily. Don't allow relational or sexual problems to become severe and chronic.

Couple identity, cooperation, and empathic communication are essential in maintaining vitality and satisfaction. Sexually, this means accepting that intimate, interactive, variable, flexible couple sexuality is more satisfying than perfect intercourse performance. Relationally, this means valuing a respectful, trusting, intimate relationship, and emotionally valuing your secure bond.

DEVELOPING YOUR COUPLE SEXUAL STYLE

Establish your unique sexual style by exploring and sharing your sexual desires, feelings, and preferences. Exercise 5.1 is divided into phases. Do the first phase individually. Then share your thoughts and reach an understanding about your couple sexuality.

• • • • • • •

EXERCISE 5.1 REFINING AND APPRECIATING YOUR COUPLE SEXUAL STYLE

Think about and then write out the answers to the following questions. Do not be "politically correct" or try to second-guess your partner. Be honest and explicit.

1. *How important is sex in your life? How important is your relationship?*
2. *In terms of affectionate touch, do you prefer kissing, holding hands, or hugging?*
3. *How much do you enjoy cuddling? How important is it to you?*
4. *How do you distinguish affectionate touch from seductive touch?*
5. *How much do you enjoy sensual touch? Do you prefer taking turns or mutual giving and receiving?*
6. *What is the meaning and value of playful touch? How comfortable are you with silly nicknames for your genitals and sexual activities?*
7. *How much do you enjoy erotic scenarios and techniques? Do you prefer single stimulation or multiple stimulation, taking turns or mutual stimulation, using external stimuli or not? Do you enjoy erotic sex as a route to orgasm or only as a pleasuring experience?*
8. *What is your preferred intercourse position: man on top, woman on top, rear entry, side to side? What type of thrusting do you prefer: in and out, circular, deep inside, fast or slow? Do you desire to engage in multiple stimulation during intercourse?*

9. *How much do you value afterplay as a part of your love-making style?*

After you have completed the questions, read your partner's responses and carefully discuss each question, clarifying both the practical and emotional dimensions.

Remember that you are not clones of each other. You want to maintain your individuality and not feel embarrassed or apologetic about your emotional and sexual desires. Your preferences and sensitivities are part of who you are as a sexual person and must be integrated into your couple style for you to be truly satisfied. Finally, divide your answers into three categories:

1. *Areas you agree on. These will enhance your enjoyment and satisfaction. For example, you both agree that you want sex to play a 15 to 20% energizing role in your relationship, and that you value verbally sharing and bonding afterplay.*
2. *Areas you can reach agreement on. Identify differences you can accept and even enjoy. The partner who more highly values sex agrees to be the initiator most of the time; one partner would rather engage in touching standing up and the other prefers sitting down; he prefers woman-on-top intercourse while she prefers side to side. You can integrate your preferences or take turns. Enjoy your partner's sexual preferences and response. Remember, an involved, aroused partner is the best aphrodisiac.*
3. *Differences to accept or adapt to. Identify areas of major differences. For example, one feels sex is the major means of connection and the other emphasizes social activities; one loves playful touching and the other hates playful touch; she wants to use a vibrator during intercourse to help her be orgasmic but he is put off by the vibrator; he wants to experiment with porn videos, which she sees as degrading to women.*

It is not easy, and can even be impossible, to integrate these differences, but there are two major coping strategies. One is to acknowledge the differences, but not let them turn into a power struggle. Instead, accept these and try to work around them. It helps to recognize that differences do not mean rejection. The second strategy is to agree to enter couple therapy to understand the meaning of the differences, and find a common ground for intimacy and sexuality.

To develop your comfortable, pleasurable, functional, and mutually satisfying couple sexual style, take personal responsibility for your sexuality and your growth as a unique, intimate team. You can be proud of yourselves for working together. Respectfully sharing emotional and sexual feelings and preferences increases understanding, empathy, and acceptance.

QUALITY COUPLE SEXUALITY: VALUING BOTH INTIMACY AND EROTICISM

Traditionally, intimacy was the woman's domain and eroticism was the man's domain. Women reacted to the man's sexual initiation focused on intercourse. The woman wasn't supposed to have her own erotic voice, and men were not supposed to be aware of intimacy needs, much less value intimacy. This traditional model is based on the mistaken assumption that women and men are totally different sexual species.

We have a substantially different concept of the emotional and sexual realities of women and men, especially those involved in a serious or marital relationship. Psychologically, relationally, and sexually there are many more similarities than differences in healthy women and men. The most important concept is that both value intimacy and eroticism, and that the common goal of sex is relationship satisfaction.

Men can and do value intimacy and touching, as do women. Women can and do value eroticism and orgasm, as do men. Rather than a war between the sexes, they have similar and complementary goals. Men and women are emotional allies who join in the pursuit of sexual satisfaction.

Intimacy and eroticism are different, but complementary, dimensions for healthy couples. Intimacy emphasizes closeness, safety, predictability, security, and a genuine, secure bond. Eroticism emphasizes high levels of emotional and sexual expression, taking personal and sexual risks, impulsivity and mystery, unpredictability, and special, energizing connection. In quality couple sexuality, both the woman and man value intimacy and eroticism, and integrate these into their chosen couple sexual style. The balance is unique to you, but both intimacy and eroticism are core components of your couple sexual style. Emotional intimacy can play a significant role in enhancing feelings that you have a secure bond and genuine connection that are safe and meaningful. Sexual intimacy also helps energize your bond and builds desire. Problems with either emotional or sexual intimacy can play an inordinately negative role in subverting relationship satisfaction and can cause a break-up.

Emotional intimacy involves sharing positive feelings and closeness. Intimacy also involves dealing with differences, emotional and practical conflicts, and sexual problem solving. A positive function of touching and sexuality is to energize you to deal with difficult issues, as well as a port in the storm in healing from conflicts and arguments.

In terms of sexual intimacy, choosing a couple style that balances intimacy and eroticism is the key developmental process after the romantic love/passionate sex phase of your relationship. Couple sexuality involves building feelings of desire, pleasure, and satisfaction. Unfortunately, it takes little for sex to degenerate into a power struggle rather than be a sharing, pleasurable, erotic experience. When sex becomes "If you really loved me, you would always say yes." Or "You need to do what I want sexually." Or the opposite extreme, "If you really loved me, you wouldn't demand sex." Or "Why can't you just hold me and feel intimate?" The phrase "If you love me, you would . . ." is a recipe for disaster. Emotionally and sexually, healthy relationships are based on a positive influence process, not demands or threats. Sex is neither a reward for good behavior nor a punishment for problem behavior.

"Intimate coercion" has no place in your couple sexual style. Contingencies, threats, coercion, and intimidation poison intimacy. You cannot be intimate friends if you are afraid of your partner. It is normal to feel disappointed, frustrated, angry, or distant on occasion, whether about sex or life issues. Touching is a positive way to heal from an argument or to stop a downward couple pattern. Sexuality is a healthy way to say you are sorry or to make up after a conflict. However, do not use arguments or physical incidents as "foreplay." Threats or incidents of interpersonal violence subvert your relationship and couple sexuality.

A satisfying, stable relationship results from being both intimate and erotic friends. A healthy intimate relationship is based on positive motivation; feeling safe and accepted; enjoying a secure, trusting bond; being receptive and responsive to pleasurable touch; being open to taking emotional and sexual risks; engaging in erotic playfulness; enjoying the intensity of sexual encounters; going with the erotic flow; valuing intercourse; letting go physically and emotionally; and delighting in the afterplay experience.

SUMMARY

Discovering and refining your couple sexual style is a core component of quality couple sexuality. To be genuinely satisfied sexually, you need to have a comfortable, pleasurable, and functional couple sexual style that balances intimacy and eroticism. This promotes a vital, resilient sexual desire that promotes satisfaction and security.

You can individualize your unique couple sexual style. Play to the strengths of your chosen style while being aware of and monitoring traps. This ensures that your couple sexuality continues to promote desire, pleasure, and satisfaction. Be sure your sexual style is flexible enough to incorporate individual preferences and changes in life circumstances. Your couple sexual style becomes even more important as you age and your relationship matures. Each style has its own way of balancing intimacy, eroticism, and sexual autonomy with being an intimate team. It is this integration and balance that ensures enduring desire and sexual satisfaction.

6

Intimate Teamwork
The Environment for GES

Sex does not exist in a vacuum. You and your partner intentionally want to create the type of environment that ensures your relationship and sexual quality

A thriving partnership is the environment for GES couple sex.

amid the moving parts of your busy lives. Careers and jobs, family, community activities, religious communities, and social networks are important features of the environment for your sexual relationship. Balancing these facets of your lives impacts sexual quality. Focusing on the deficits in this balancing act is self-defeating. Thinking of unavoidable stresses as "problems," disagreements as "power struggles," or responsibilities as "burdens" will misdirect you into gloom and unhappiness.

This is an unhealthy environment for your sex life. Sexually vibrant couples cooperate; they work as an intimate team. Healthy couples are committed to a process of growing relationship and sexual quality, not neglecting or taking either for granted.

Take a broader perspective and consider how well you are nurturing your overall relationship. A thriving partnership is the environment for GES couple sex. Partners who feel lonely, taken for granted, resentful, unappreciated, bored, or blamed have huge barriers to GES and sexual satisfaction.

RELATIONSHIP SKILLS

Three essential components promote the environment for your vital and satisfying sexual life:

1. Value your relationship as unique, with its own special *identity* or personality. This involves balancing the composite of cognitive features such as: the meaning of your interactions, a blend of individual autonomy and relationship cohesion, gender roles, and parenting values.
2. Emphasize *cooperation*, how you handle your disagreements. Conflicts are normal. They can be incidental (inconveniences, pet-peeves) or major (value conflicts). They provide a built-in opportunity to deepen your intimacy, including sexual intimacy. Conflict provides the energy—autonomy within cohesion—that fuels your sexual desire.
3. Cultivate mutual *empathy*, the "emotional embrace" that constitutes the vital glue of your relationship.

When confused, frustrated, or anxious about your relationship—in or out of the bedroom—consider the source of your misunderstandings, snagged conflict patterns, or deficits in empathy. Friction or disconnect in any one of the three relationship skill dimensions reverberates into the other two. For example, if you are having trouble appreciating each other's perspectives or difficulty operating as a team, it can manifest as a deficit in emotional empathy, which infringes further on your cooperation and identity. These difficulties are common and fuel debate and defensiveness rather than calmly listening to and reflecting your partner's feelings before focusing on what happened or what to do. Consider your partner's feelings when dealing with conflict, understand differences in the meaning, and discuss how to get on the same page.

*Connecting the Dots: Relationship Features
and Your Sexual Interactions*

The three relationship areas influence your psychosexual skills—the cognitive, behavioral, and emotional (C-B-E) dimensions of sexuality. You have a powerful resource for satisfying sex when you appreciate the connections between understanding your relationship thoughts and feelings, interactions outside the bedroom, and sexual attitudes and desire. For example, when you believe that couple cohesion is undermined by your partner's independence (autonomy), you feel hurt and pull away from touch because you mistakenly believe that sex is mechanical, that you are being used or placated, or that sex is for your partner—not you as a couple. This meaning follows from your assumption ("sex should always be wild and passionate"), perception ("partner is too independent"), attribution ("our cohesion is undermined"), and subsequent meaning ("mechanical," "used," sex only for partner). Saddled with this negativity, it is understandable that you feel hurt and respond by pulling away. On the other hand, if you accept that your partner's autonomy is important for her or him to feel independent, then you seek to balance autonomy and cohesion by physical connection. When you consider that your partner may think or feel differently than you do, you bring flexibility to your sexual interactions and your partner relationship.

ENHANCING RELATIONSHIP IDENTITY

Relationship identity involves your beliefs, standards, assumptions, and attributions about your relationship, lifestyle, and sexuality. To what extent are you and your partner in agreement? Remember that differences in thinking are common. Integrating these differences into your relationship identity is part of adaptation, appreciating your partner's individuality, and promoting your quality relationship environment. Complete Exercise 6.1 to appraise your relationship identity.

• • • • • • •

EXERCISE 6.1 EXPLORING YOUR RELATIONSHIP IDENTITY AREAS

Using a 10-point scale, with 0 indicating "no agreement" and 10 indicating "complete agreement," assess the degree of similarity and difference in the way you regard your relationship identity areas. In what areas are you on the same page?

Identity Area	Degree of consensus (0 = none; 10 = complete)
1. Accepting personal differences	
2. Individual independence or autonomy	
3. The degree of cohesion or closeness you want in your relationship	
4. Degree of structure or organization in your personal, family, and home life	
5. Degree of spontaneity in your couple life	
6. Beliefs about sexual fidelity	
7. Privacy boundaries regarding your couple life with parents, relatives, and friends	
8. Privacy boundaries about your sex life	
9. Parenting styles and how to praise and punish your children	
10. How to resolve couple conflicts	
11. How to handle finances	
12. Type of religious participation	
13. Where to live and whether to rent or buy	
14. The kind of job(s) you have	
15. How many hours you work	
16. Whether to have children and how many	
17. Whether you value a "stay-at-home" parent for your children	
18. When to have sex	
19. How to have sex	
20. Whether you pray together and how	
21. Talking about your future, philosophy of life, or "the meaning of life"	
22. How and when to pursue personal interests versus couple time	

(Continued)

Identity Area	Degree of consensus (0 = none; 10 = complete)
23. When and where to take vacations	
24. Responsibilities for caring for your aging parents	
25. How much time to spend with your individual friends	

Hopefully you and your partner agree on many areas. Value your consensus because this comprises a crucial component of your relationship identity. Discuss those items in which you differ in order to understand each other's perspective. Discuss how to get "on the same page" as a team (rather than debate issues) and how to accept differences you can't merge. The essence of conflict involves your relationship identity—differences in the meanings you each bring to a topic of dispute. Do not let differences polarize you, which happens when differences are inflamed by thoughts of rejection or belittlement, leading to adversarial debates. Or the other extreme, avoidance and dismissal of negative feelings fosters resentment, distance, lifeless sex, and, in many cases, loss of sexual desire. Understanding and respecting each other's views of your relationship identity is essential for cooperating as an "intimate team."

QUALITY SEX IS BASED ON RELATIONSHIP COOPERATION

Couples tend to handle conflict in the bedroom similarly to outside-the-bedroom issues. For example, couples who discuss issues outside the bedroom calmly, with empathy and mutual cooperation, tend to deal with sexual difficulties in an empathetic, cooperative manner. On the other hand, couples who avoid relationship conflict also avoid dealing with sexual difficulties. Couples who argue intensely about general issues tend to fight intensely about sexual issues. Sex difficulties are often more intense (whether addressed or avoided) because sex is so personal and emotional.

A common notion is that couples who have conflicts are in trouble and will eventually divorce. This may or may not be true depending on the manner in which they deal with conflict. Aggression, blame-counterblame, personal attacks, and "trash-talk" are common among couples who divorce. The issue is not whether you have conflict, but rather *how* you address it. Do you attack and try to hurt your partner (aggression)? Do you avoid conflict or "stick your head in the sand" (evasion)? Do you always give in (yield)? Or do you talk things out and work through the issues (cooperation)? Working cooperatively as an "intimate team" allows you to achieve positive and mutually satisfying conflict resolution.

Many couples are able to use sexual intimacy to help them heal from conflicts. These couples place their cohesion above winning or staying committed to resentment. Healthy conflict resolution is an exquisite

> **Debating, arguing, fighting, and withdrawal indicate an impasse and failure to cooperate.**

cognitive-behavioral-emotional skill. Other couples, with positive intentions, try to "protect" their sexual relationship from unresolved conflict by partitioning conflict from sex. However, this creates a mood barrier to relaxation and sexual pleasure. Cooperation and mutual resolution of conflict is crucial to sexual satisfaction. GES is grounded on realistic expectations about couple conflict. A better approach to conflict resolution is mutual emotional understanding and accommodation. The focus is on both partners feeling emotionally satisfied with how they manage conflict.

While this is not always achievable, it is the gold standard that can inspire sexual desire, excitement, and satisfaction.

Protect Your Bedroom with Cooperation

If you are fighting about an issue—sexual or otherwise—and cannot manage or resolve it, or if you are highly avoidant, it is likely that alienated feelings will end up in the bedroom. Arguing, fighting, debating, and withdrawal indicate an impasse and failure to find the constructive way to cooperate. Unresolved conflict invariably affects feelings and behaviors, including emotional contempt, an attitude of victimization, frustration, anger, loneliness, and bitterness. These feelings can precipitate sexual avoidance and loneliness, and can deepen sexual conflict, alienation, and resentment.

The Role of Conflict in Relationship and Sexual Satisfaction

Appreciate that conflict is normal, and that conflict resolution is the optimal way in which couples deepen their personal understanding. Addressing conflict plays a powerful role in sexual intimacy. If conflict is unresolved (that is, if both partners do not come away

> **When you deal well with your conflict, you feel respected and special in your partner's eyes.**

feeling well), it provokes negative feelings and is likely to inhibit other avenues of intimacy such as positive communication, parental cooperation, recreation, and sharing of projects.

On the other hand, when conflicts are satisfactorily managed, the emotional confidence and trust created by mutual conflict resolution becomes a source of energy for sexual desire.

Healthy couples realize that when partners disagree and calmly explain (without debate) their perspectives about sex, parenting, work demands, relatives, household tasks, or vacation plans in constructive ways, they learn more about each other, their thoughts and emotions and why they act and react the way they do. These couples use conflict as a way to deepen couple intimacy. Cooperating and accommodating constitute the path to empathy—the premier feeling that grounds respect, trust, and intimacy. These are the bonding energies you want to take to your bedroom.

In healthy relationships, disagreements are a catalyst for intimacy. When you deal well with conflict, you feel respected and special in your partner's eyes. When feelings of trust and cooperation linger in your bedroom, they generate proud feelings and a loving environment that foster long-term sexual desire and function. Sexual health, passion, and satisfaction are directly influenced by relationship cooperation, shared empathy, and mutual conflict resolution (Metz & Epstein, 2002).

Beware of Poisonous Patterns

Life is not perfect. Real people face a number of challenges and difficulties that they need to balance, prevent, or correct in their relationship interactions. If you or your relationship chronically experience the subversive and painful patterns that follow, it is wise to seek individual and/or couple therapy. Resources for finding a competent therapist are in Appendix A.

Personal Scars and Traumas   You bring to your relationship a personal legacy of entitlement or privilege, on the one hand, or painful experiences such as childhood physical abuse, neglect, or sexual abuse, on the other. These can contribute to sexual problems and distress. Such scars may result in discontent, tension, and hurt, which decrease the sense of intimacy and cohesion that otherwise would allow you to embrace relationship conflict together. In addition, individuals who grew up in families characterized by stressful experiences such as substance abuse or poverty are at increased risk for adult relationship problems.

Psychological Vulnerabilities Relationship conflict can stem from characteristics of one or both partners, including personality quirks, psychopathology, and dysfunctional family of origin experiences. Some partners have personality characteristics that directly interfere with sexual functioning and thereby affect their overall relationship. For example, individuals with panic disorder can fear bodily sensations of arousal (Barlow, 1988), including those associated with sexual arousal with their partner (Sbrocco, Weisberg, Barlow, & Carter, 1997). Even when both partners intellectually understand that the anxiety disorder is unrelated to sexual attraction, your partner's inhibited sexual responsiveness can contribute to relationship conflict and distress. Understanding that the dysfunction is beyond the individual's control may not be sufficient to maintain intimacy and minimize relationship conflict. These problems often require psychotherapy and sometimes medications to adapt to physical and psychological challenges (see Appendix A).

Even when neither partner has any notable vulnerabilities that interfere with his or her functioning, you still may experience conflict based on marked differences in your needs, preferences, or personality styles. Couples who lack the ability to constructively communicate about and negotiate such differences are likely to develop distressing levels of conflict.

Harmful Couple Interaction Patterns There are several paths by which relationship conflict can lead to sexual problems. One path involves ongoing negative moods, resulting in nasty, aversive, or disgusted feelings—what researchers call negative *sentiment override* (Weiss, 1980). In this case, conflict leads each partner to experience over-arching negative emotions and attitudes. If the mere presence of your partner elicits negative affect, that emotion interferes with sexual desire and function. These negative moods commonly develop over time when emotional kindness or empathy is lacking.

A second path that can beget sexual problems involves negative filters—*interaction narrowing* (Gottman, 1994). These filters blind you to the bigger picture, so unresolved conflict narrows the way you behave toward each other. Your interactions become automatic and repetitive. Harmful behavioral patterns dominate and replace interactions that were intimate, seductive, or sexually inviting.

Related to negative filtering is a chronic conflict focus on control and power because you feel a need to protect yourself from being manipulated, hurt, or abused. Earlier in the relationship you interacted in ways that met your intimacy needs. Now you focus on interactions that are self-protective and even controlling. When strong conflictual interactions occur, it takes a lot of positives to balance them. The negatives are very vivid stimuli that are emotionally intense, dominate your perceptions, and elicit self-protective withdrawal or aggressive responses. Power struggles are essentially cooperation problems.

Another self-defeating pattern is blame-counterblame—*negative reciprocity* (Bradbury & Fincham, 1990). When partners play the "blame game" and respond to relationship conflict with a pattern of attack and counter-attack that involves reciprocating negative acts with criticism and threats, they escalate relationship distress. You wrongly feel your automatic negative behavior is warranted by the situation. You deny your own negative behavior, and justify your part by saying you don't intend to destroy cooperation, that it's your partner's fault. Reciprocal blame is maintained by the negative cognitions (attributions) that you have about each other's feelings and intentions—which, although often inaccurate, fuel yet more negative communication.

Why Negative Communication Patterns Are Anti-Sexual

Negative cognitions and behaviors are a sexual "turn-off," the antithesis of a nurturing environment for quality sexuality. They subvert positive emotional, cognitive, and behavioral aspects of couple sexuality and

> "No one wants to make love to a cactus."

may cause sex dysfunction (low sexual desire, arousal dysfunction, orgasm dysfunction).

They hurt, alienate, and push you away from each other. One person poignantly lamented, "No one wants to make love to a cactus."

Changing this situation requires your intentional decision to monitor and regulate your negative thoughts, feelings, and behaviors, and to use communication skills for mutual empathy. If negative patterns are affecting your sexual feelings, consider talking to your partner about the situation in a calm, cooperative tone. If this does not help you work as a team to improve, seek a couple therapist who can facilitate your exploration and cooperation (Appendix A).

The following case illustrates Tracy and Mark's negative communication process and highlights their distressing cognitions (C), behaviors (B), and emotions (E). Use the questions at the end to discuss and learn.

TRACY AND MARK

Mark's chronic lateness coming home from work (B) led Tracy to think of him as selfish, dismissive, and rejecting of her childcare stresses (C). She felt hurt (E) that her feelings were dismissed (C). One evening when he came home 35 minutes late, she said "Where have you been?" (B), which Mark took as "criticism" (C) and sharply responded, "At work!" Tracy expressed her frustration to have the kids underfoot while trying to prepare dinner saying, "Mark, sometimes you are so inconsiderate!" Mark did not intend (C) to be so. Rather, he felt burdened as the principal financial provider as Tracy worked part-time so she could stay home 3 days a week with their two small children. He felt deeply hurt (E), and thought he was not appreciated (C). Mark believed he "always upset" Tracy (C) and was a "failure" (C) as a husband. He feared disappointing Tracy, predicting "there will be hell to pay" (C). In his frustration and hurt (E), he disengaged (B), which appeared to Tracy as (C) hostile, insensitive to her needs, and reinforcing her hurt and irritation(E).

When Mark addressed conflict, he'd apologize to try to deflect his attribution (C) that Tracy was critiquing him. Then he stopped further discussion and became quiet (B). He felt ashamed (E) to think he disappointed his wife (C) and was frustrated with himself (E). When Tracy's criticism became too much (E), Mark would lash back and call her names (B).

All of these actions (B) seemed to Tracy to be insensitive (C) to her wants and feelings, deeply hurtful (E), and an abandonment (C) that was hard to interpret as anything but disregard for her efforts at work, in the home, and in their relationship (C). Her hurt and frustration (E) was compounded by her "knowing" (C) that Mark would not listen and avoided her. Her hurt (E) was manifested as complaints, criticisms, and expressions of anger (B), even rage at times. Confronted with Tracy's behavior, Mark felt betrayed (E). He misunderstood (C) Tracy's "criticism" (B) as a lack of appreciation and support (C) when "I have to do my job or we don't eat!" (B).

Mark was irritated (E) and confused (C) about what to do (B). He thought the situation was completely hopeless (C) and pulled away (B) in hurt and frustration (E). He saw himself in a double-bind (C): "Stand up to her and it's a big fight; leave it alone and she acts worse." Tracy's double-bind (C): "If I say anything, he gets mad or goes away; but if I say nothing, it can't get better." The cycle took on a life of its own. Mark and Tracy felt polarized and were no longer intimate friends.

Based on Mark and Tracy's example, consider and discuss:

1. What are the differences between each partner's intentions and perceptions?
2. How and where could Tracy and Mark interrupt the negative cycle and salvage their dysfunctional interaction?
3. Track Tracy's cognitions/emotions/behaviors: What do you learn?
4. Track Mark's cognitions/emotions/ behaviors: What do you learn?
5. What is the impact of this conflict on their sex life?
6. What could Tracy and Mark do to heal from their conflict? How might they work together? How might the effect you envision help their sexual relationship?
7. Does this example raise awareness of your own relationship dynamics and how you view each other as intimate and sexual friends?
8. What did you learn that can apply to yourselves?

Conflict Presents Opportunities for Deeper Intimacy

Disagreements present opportunities to deepen your emotional and sexual intimacy. With a positive, respectful, affirming process of conflict resolution, you can reinforce respect and admiration for each other, develop confidence that future conflict can be resolved, and create positive feelings and comfort that facilitate sexual desire. The crucial feature is the *meaning* of your conflict. First, what attributions underlie the meaning of the conflict for you? What does it signify to you? What underlies your frustration? Why do you feel this so strongly? Does it signify that you are feeling unloved. rejected, unimportant, a low priority to your partner?

Next, consider how you are dealing with the discord. Positive and constructive interaction can produce emotional relief and even affirm your intimate bond. Directly or indirectly, this can serve as a sexual aphrodisiac. The heightened pleasure and enjoyment that couples report when they have make-up sex after resolving conflict affirmatively offers further evidence of the emotional link between conflict resolution and sexual feelings.

Explore the meanings of your conflict with Exercise 6.2.

• • • • • • •

EXERCISE 6.2 CONSIDER THE MEANINGS
OF YOUR RELATIONSHIP CONFLICTS

How well do you and your partner understand the meaning of your disagreements and how to handle them? Consider the following:

1. *What thoughts typically go through your mind about your partner and the issues when you are having a disagreement?*
2. *What is upsetting about the fact that you have a disagreement in this particular area?*
3. *Are your interactions similar or different from what you experienced with your family when you were growing up?*

4. *Describe ways in which conflicts are based on having different beliefs about how your relationship should be.*
5. *What do you expect will result when you discuss important relationship topics?*
6. *Ideally, what would happen when you disagree about an area of your relationship?*
7. *What is the underlying, hidden meaning of your conflict? For example, "My partner doesn't care about my feelings"; "My partner takes me for granted." These are your attributions and are likely to be inaccurate; talk with your partner to check out your attributions.*
8. *When your sex life is less vital or satisfying for you or your partner, what does this mean?*
9. *When your sex life is energized and vital, what does this indicate? When it is unexciting and tedious, what does this signify?*
10. *What would ultimately help you feel satisfied when a conflict occurs?*

Work Out Your Disagreements: Bridge-Blend-Bond

A tool to help you resolve differences is the "Bridge, Blend, and Bond" method. Working as a team, you:

1. *Bridge your differences* by calmly listening to and understanding (not debating) each other so you appreciate your different meanings.
2. *Blend your meanings* in a way that respects and integrates the thoughts and feelings of both you and your partner.
3. *Bond with your partner* through valuing your intimate teamwork.

An example: One partner arrives home late from work without a call, and the other is irritated and brusquely says so. Recognizing the tension, they cooperate by agreeing to postpone talking on the spot, but set a time for discussion after they have dealt with the kids and dinner. Later, as agreed, they take time to bridge-blend-bond. Each *bridges* by taking turns to briefly explain the underlying meaning and feelings the lateness triggered. For one person, it meant inconsiderateness and felt unloving. For the other, it meant being unsupported and unappreciated for hard work. In bridging, it is not a matter of right or wrong, accuracy, or fairness, but sharing and accepting each other's perception of the situation.

Blending involves each understanding the other's meaning, and then working together to figure out how to deal with it in the future in a way that makes both partners feel good. Sometimes it may be enough to simply share and understand the difference in meanings: "I just want you to understand . . . ." At other times it may involve working out a specific way to handle these situations. This might entail phoning ahead when running late, a 15-minute "benefit-of-the-doubt" margin, or a "penalty" if the agreement is violated, such as doing something the other wants to "make it right." When couples blend, it reinforces the notion that cooperation is more important than negative interpretations (attribution) and division.

The *bonding* that can result makes the emotional work worth it. It requires a combination of courage and patience to use this method; but when you bridge, blend, and bond your differences, you block hurt, bitterness, and resentment, and instead promote respectful, warm, and united feelings. This is what we mean by "conflict is an opportunity for growth in intimacy." Cooperating in this way can enhance sexual energy and ignite desire.

THE PREMIER RELATIONSHIP SKILL: EMPATHY

When your relationship identity and cooperation are good enough (not perfect), these valued sources merge to enhance emotional intimacy. If your couple identity and cooperation are deficient, emotional empathy—the premier emotional skill—is blocked.

The word "empathy" comes from the Greek language, "e" meaning "from" and "pathos" meaning "emotion." Empathy means that you take the feeling "from" your partner and feel it with him or her. Empathy involves imagining what your partner feels with understanding and compassion. When you listen to your partner's ideas and feelings, you seek to accept that this is what he or she thinks (perceives, interprets, attributes) and feels (positive versus. negative energy). It is not a matter of facts, accuracy, or fairness but accepting the thoughts and feelings without debating or challenging your partner. Empathy is not about agreement. When you disagree, judge, or debate your partner, he or she will inevitably interpret your actions as rejection. This dysfunctional interactional pattern harms many well-intentioned relationships.

It is wise to walk in your partner's shoes and view a situation through your partner's eyes. Accept her or his ideas and feelings, try them on, then reflect back on what you are hearing. You don't have to agree. Empathy is checking out whether your perceptions and impressions fit, not whether they're right or wrong. To empathize with your lover does not mean you agree or endorse his or her meaning. You want to fully understand your partner's thoughts and feelings. Do not insist on rectitude, fairness, or sameness. Empathy is the glue of a good relationship.

The Paraphrasing Tool for Empathy

When there is a conflict, empathy is the default mode you need. Without empathy as the foundation for decisions about action, your problem-solving choices—however smart—might fail because they are not molded to the concept of ensuring each partner feels accepted—the foundation of an intimate team.

> Empathy is the solid foundation from which partners resolve conflicts.

Conflict resolutions that fail are usually ones that ignore empathy and undermine relationship satisfaction.

"Paraphrasing" (Figure 6.1), an excellent skill that promotes empathy, involves three steps: (1) one partner offers an "I" message, (2) the other partner "paraphrases" it, and (3) the partner who

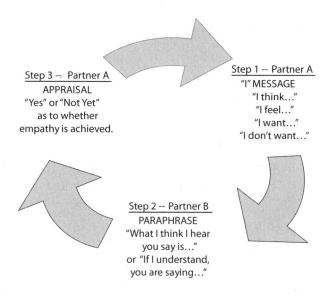

Figure 6.1 The empathy process.

offered the "I" message appraises empathy. If empathy is not veri-
fied (a "not-yet" appraisal), the "I" message is rephrased to make it
clearer. When used with skillful care, these steps prevent common
communication mistakes and promote emotional connection.

Commonly, misunderstandings and hurt result from deficits
in the paraphrasing process. For example, misunderstandings do
not start with an "I" message (constructive focus on the speaker)
but rather with a "you" message: "You aren't listening to me" or
"It's your fault." This shifts focus to the listener, which sets up
defensiveness, the opposite of empathy; this is where the communication process turns negative and falters. When this process
occurs frequently, you begin to predict—unfortunately and incor-
rectly—that there is no way your partner is going to understand
your feelings and no point in trying to communicate. Empathy is
vanquished and alienation and pessimism set in.

Empathy is the solid foundation from which you resolve conflicts. When your mutual decision incorporates your hidden
meanings and desired feelings into the agreement, the plan will
be successful. When both partners feel good about the decision,

this agreement is self-sustaining: a win-win strategy. When your team identity, cooperation, empathy, and mutually satisfying conflict resolution are well blended, you're building the environment to promote GES. With this anchor, your GES growth goals can flourish and ensure sexual satisfaction.

Making Empathy Tangible

You can create powerful verbal empathy with skills such as paraphrasing. Are there times you've thought, "I just want you to understand me; you don't have to agree or do what I want. Just understand!" This signals your desire for empathy. Empathy is even more strongly shared when you make it physically tangible with nonsexual touch. We all long for both verbal and physical empathy to confirm caring. If this relationship glue is wanting, it inevitably restricts your sexual well-being.

Appreciate that we have "skin hunger"—our bodies have this longing for hugs, comforting touch, and caresses as both children and adults. Without physical touch, we can feel alienated, lonely, neglected.

Verbal and physical empathy certify caring.

We are more assured and confident when we receive human touch from our partner (see Chapter 9).

Affectionate touch refers to the day-to-day gestures of closeness such as kissing, warm gestures of caring and fondness, hugging, and holding hands to reinforce feelings of intimacy and connection.

Comfort/compassionate touch refers to consoling and soothing embrace, reassuring, supportive, and calm touch that is often outside the bedroom. When the vicissitudes of life occur (major disappointments, a child hurt in an accident, illnesses, death, unusual challenges, and other sufferings), you "step up" and give your partner tangible, physical support through touch. When you are suffering, you know you can count on receiving this benefit of loving in your relationship. Comfort touch is nonsexual touch that gives gentle acceptance, sympathy, and reassurance when you need a safe harbor or a pillar of support.

Such touch is essential to your intimate team. Making empathy tangible with affectionate and compassionate touch creates feelings of connection that inspire and energize your sexual activities (see details in Chapter 9). Contrary to common societal stereotypes, men as well as women want and need tangible empathy. Where words fail, a strong embrace or gentle human touch communicates concern, understanding, acceptance, caring, and support.

Your Environment for Eroticism

Your shared identity, realistic cooperation in dealing with life's responsibilities, your tangible empathy and its physical comfort, generate your climate for couple sex (Figure 6.2). A vital, erotic sexual relationship reciprocally provides special pleasures and high-quality feelings that promote cooperation, shared identity, and mutual empathy.

A common false assumption in our society is that a solid relationship guarantees sexual desire and satisfaction. Both factors—intimacy and eroticism—are necessary; one without the other is not sufficient. Over time, deficits in intimacy or eroticism will

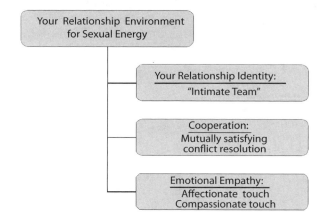

Figure 6.2 Your relationship environment.

undermine your couple satisfaction. Ensure lifelong satisfaction with dedication to strong intimacy and robust eroticism.

GES is grounded on relationship teamwork both in and outside the bedroom. Your relationship identity, cooperation, and empathy are the environment for sexual desire, special pleasure, eroticism, and satisfaction. You bring your feelings as an intimate team to the bedroom, which forms the foundation for lustful, passionate, touch, sensuality, pleasure, eroticism, intercourse, orgasm— for high-quality GES.

SUMMARY

When your couple environment is strong, you've created the climate for sexual vitality. When your relationship is sexually vital, it creates and enhances the environment for relationship intimacy. Healthy couples balance these two crucial dimensions as an intimate team that relies on understanding and empathy to resolve differences. When your relationship is strong, you can face and weather all types of crises, buoyed by the knowledge that you have a source of strong, resilient love and support. This partnership provides the environment for your thriving sexual energy and, in turn, your sexual vitality promotes and sustains your identity, cooperation, and empathy as an intimate team.

7

Celebrating Your Sexual Being
Confident Sex

You and your partner have a right to feel proud of your body and your sexuality. When you feel proud of your bodies, you bring confidence to your

> You have a right to feel proud of your body and your sexuality.

sex life. You do not need a perfect body to have great sex. Sexual function is important (although not essential) for sexual satisfaction. Caring for your physical health and healthy behaviors (e.g., adequate sleep, exercise, eating, moderate drinking) is an important dimension of sexual function at every age. Because illness is a significant enemy of sexual function, and can be more prevalent as we age, wellness is a crucial goal.

With recent medical advances, including medications (Testosterone, Viagra, Levitra, Cialis) and physical devices such as female vacuum devices (e.g., Eros) and male erectile vacuum devices (e.g., Erecaid), you can facilitate sexual functioning. However, these need to be integrated into your couple sexual style, not used as "stand-alone" interventions (McCarthy & Fucito, 2005).

VALUING SEX AS INHERENTLY GOOD

Essential to the GES approach is to value sex as inherently good. Men and women who develop sexual problems usually do not value their sexual body, lack sexual confidence, underestimate the power of their sex drive, and minimize their desire for emotional intimacy (Cooper & Marcus, 2003). Negative cognitions (Boul, 2007; Fichten, Spector, & Libman, 1988) link sex with embarrassment, even shame, and compartmentalize sex from real life. Sex-positive therapy (Kleinplatz, 1996) facilitates acceptance of sexuality and honors sex as a means for you to use your body for fun, pleasure, affirmation, and closeness. Developing sexual self-esteem—the antithesis of shame—requires accepting and affirming sexuality, respecting honest sexual feelings, regulating sexual behaviors, and promoting self-esteem. Sexual self-esteem requires understanding, accepting, and respecting your body and emotional and sexual desires.

Satisfying sex begins with embracing your sexuality, appreciating the built-in personal sex-drive imperative (Fisher, Aron, Mashek, Haifang, & Brown, 2002), and the contribution of sexual satisfaction for you and your relationship. It is well-documented that fears of sex, disgust, or shame-based notions are serious barriers to sexual health and satisfaction. For example, sexual shame is implicated in chemical dependency (O'Farrell, Choquette, Cutter, & Birchler, 1997) and sexual dysfunction (LaPera, Giannotti, Taggi, Macchia, 2003). Sexually satisfied couples confront negative notions involving their bodies and value sex as inherently good.

Placing a strong, positive value on sex, each other's body, and the joys of shared sex is essential for individual and couple sexual confidence. Confidence fuels long-term comfort, pleasure, eroticism, and satisfaction.

MIND AND BODY

The biopsychosocial model of healthy male, female, and couple sexuality builds on the perspective that sex is an integral, positive part of your life as individuals and as a couple.

> **Good physical health and healthy behavioral habits are vital for your sexual health.**

Sexuality is an excellent example of an integrated mind-body approach. You cannot understand sexuality by just examining biological/medical dimensions of your body. Carefully appreciate the biological, psychological, and relational factors that subvert sexual health. Even more important, you want to understand how biological, psychological, and relational factors interact to promote your sexual health.

Understanding and accepting your physical body and how it functions forms the foundation for being accepting and proud of your sexual body. When men think of their sexual body, they focus almost all their attention on their penis. In fact, your sexual body is much more than your penis. It is crucial to accept your body rather than be driven by hype and unrealistic performance expectations. A statistic to illustrate the self-defeating performance comparison is that more than 75% of men worry that their penis is smaller than average. In addition to making no statistical sense, this makes no psychological sense. What is the truth about penis size? There are differences in the flaccid size of the penis, but that has very little to do with penis size or sexual function in the erect state. The average penis is from two and a half to four inches in the flaccid state and from five and a half to six and a half inches when erect. That is the scientific reality.

So why does this information not reduce the superstition and misinformation that is so rampant, especially among younger males? Men stubbornly perpetuate penis myths because they are afraid to challenge the sexual folklore of what it means to be a "real man." Younger females struggle with confronting the myths of breast size, weight, and attractiveness or what it means to be a "real woman." Sexual self-confidence is a more powerful aphrodisiac than body parts. It is "what you do with what you've got" that inspires your sex life.

BODY IMAGE AND SEXUAL CONFIDENCE

Psychological and sexual health is promoted by adopting a positive body image. For men, the science is clear; there is no rela-

> Sexual self-confidence is a more powerful aphrodisiac than body parts.

tionship between penis size and sexual desire. Most importantly, almost all penises allow the man and woman to have successful intercourse.

There is no relationship between penis size and sexual response for either the man or the woman. Most women do not understand the man's obsession with penis size; her focus is on quality and the interactive process of lovemaking.

A related myth is that a larger penis results in the woman achieving orgasm during intercourse. This is based on the mistaken belief that the vagina is the woman's major sex organ. In truth, a woman's most sensitive sex organ is her clitoris, which is located at the top of the vaginal opening and retracts under the clitoral hood. The clitoris has a multitude of erotic nerve endings. Most women prefer indirect clitoral stimulation with the hand, tongue, or penis. During intercourse, a woman's clitoris is stimulated by the pulling and rubbing action caused by penile thrusting (again, not affected by penis size). The most important thing to understand about the vagina is that it is an active, not passive, organ. A woman's vagina swells and expands with arousal and adjusts to the penis, regardless of size. Sexual dysfunction based on the couple's genitals is, with extremely rare exceptions, a myth.

OUR SEXUAL BODIES

Most of us as we grow up learn the basics about our sexual anatomy—vagina, erections, orgasm, penis—in school health or physical education classes. However, it is quite uncommon that you are given information about how women's and men's bodies function sexually (sexual physiology), how our bodies "work," what to do to enhance pleasure, function, and confidence. Most of us are left to figure things out on our own, often garnering impressions from other kids, rumors, television shows, pop music, maybe books or pornography (Exercise 7.1).

• • • • • • •

EXERCISE 7.1 REMEMBERING HOW AND WHAT YOU LEARNED ABOUT SEX

Our attitudes toward our bodies and sexuality are strongly influenced by what and how we learned as children, adolescents, and young adults. Most children receive no clear verbal messages from parents about sex. Nevertheless, attitudes are formed by the lack of messages. For example, when parents evade sexual teaching opportunities, a common childhood interpretation is that "sex must be bad, shameful" so we can't talk about it. Studies in the U.S. suggest that less than 40% of parents provide sex education for their children. At the same time, more than 75% of young kids "play doctor" to explore bodies. Schools offer some sex education, although often limited to anatomy.

Consider how you learned about sex as a child. Sex is taboo? Sex is wonderful? Sex is bad? Sex is a normal part of life? Sex is for pleasure? Sex is for baby-making? Sex is for love between two committed adults? Sex is _____?

The important issue is what did you learn to value regarding:

- *Your body*
- *Your partner's body*
- *Masturbation*
- *Sexual touch*
- *Sex in relationship*
- *Intercourse*
- *Oral sex*
- *Eroticism*

The GES yardstick is that in married or serious relationships, there are many more emotional and sexual similarities than differences between women and men. The challenge is to be both intimate and erotic friends and choose a couple sexual style that is comfortable and functional for both of you. There are clear biological/physiological differences that need to be understood and honored by both partners.

CHALLENGES FOR MEN

You are a sexual being from the day you are born until the day you die. Sexual response is a normal, natural physiological process. Your sexual body is more than just your penis, and sexuality is more than an erection, intercourse, and orgasm. Your whole body is sexual. Your most important sexual organ is your mind, which allows you to anticipate and value sex. As you age, your vascular and neurological systems remain functional, but become less efficient. This is not an illness, but a normal physiological process of aging. As a teenager and young adult, you experienced sexual response as easy, highly predictable, totally in your control, and most important, autonomous. In other words, you could experience desire, arousal, and orgasm without needing anything from your partner. Rather than viewing this as a physiological developmental phase and being open to the next developmental phase of intimate, interactive couple sexuality, your mind betrays you and sets you up for sexual dysfunction. You mistakenly believe autonomous, perfect intercourse performance is the only "right" kind of sex, and anything less is a failure. That's why understanding the biopsychosocial model and having positive, realistic sexual expectations become so crucial.

A major struggle for male sexuality is dealing with performance expectations. The biological challenge for you is to accept that your whole body is sexual and to identify body parts that are receptive and responsive to sensual and sexual touch. This can include awareness of sensual feelings when your chest or back are stroked, when your head is rubbed, when you rub your body against your partner's or give sensual touch. Sexually and erotically, many men are responsive to testicle or buttock stimulation, to receiving manual or oral penile stimulation, and "piggy-backing" their arousal on their partner's arousal. Psychologically, the challenge is to embrace the variable, flexible GES model rather than view this as "second-class" sex. Intimate, interactive sexuality is quality sex for real-life couples. Don't cling to the perfect intercourse performance model. Relationally, awareness and understanding of your body's pattern of sexual receptivity and responsivity, as well as your partner's unique pattern of sexual receptivity and responsivity, are crucial for quality couple sexuality.

CHALLENGES FOR WOMEN

As a woman, what are the special challenges for you and your sexual body? There are two guidelines: female genitalia and response are more variable and complex than for males (not better or worse, but different), and most women learn sexual response as intimate and interactive, not autonomous.

The sexuality struggle for females is dealing with old repressive myths, as well as new magical myths. You have the capacity for lifelong desire, arousal, and satisfaction. In terms of sexual function, 25-year-old-women are more functional than 20-year-old women, and 35-year-old-women are more functional than 25-year-old women. The message of this data is that with maturity, you develop an affirming "sexual voice" and, together with your intimate partner, create a mutually satisfying couple sexual style that integrates intimacy and eroticism.

Biologically, the clitoris is your major sexual organ, although many women also report strong erotic sensations from vulva, breast, vaginal, and buttock stimulation. In addition, women have more capacity for multi-orgasmic response. Biologically, as well as psychologically and in terms of psychosexual skills, a helpful concept is accepting complexity and variability of sexual response. For example, some women are orgasmic with breast stimulation alone, while other women find breast stimulation aversive. About 50% of women are responsive to oral stimulation (especially when already aroused), while others find receiving oral stimulation makes them self-conscious. Many women enjoy giving stimulation as a means to heighten their arousal while others do not. Another factor is the variability and complexity of orgasmic response. The old myth was the primacy of "vaginal orgasm" and the inferiority of "clitoral orgasm." If the old myths were repressive, the new myths are oppressive. They focus on magical performance goals: "G-spot" orgasms, "superior" multiple orgasmic response, extended orgasm, and the need for orgasm at each sexual encounter.

What is the scientific truth about female orgasm, and what are the personally relevant guidelines for women? The key guidelines are acceptance that arousal is not automatic, respect for variability, and valuing your unique preference for orgasmic response. Orgasm is a healthy, integral component of female sexuality. Approximately one in four women has an orgasmic pattern similar to the male pattern—a single orgasm during intercourse without additional stimulation. For the two in three who have orgasm during intercourse, the key is multiple stimulation during intercourse (including his, her, or vibrator clitoral stimulation; use of erotic fantasies; breast or buttock stimulation). A very important scientific finding is that one in three women are never or very rarely orgasmic during intercourse itself. The orgasmic pattern for these women is with manual, oral, rubbing, or vibrator stimulation. This is a normal, healthy orgasmic pattern, not a sexual dysfunction (Heiman, 2007).

So what does this information mean for quality couple sexuality? You need to be aware of your own unique arousal/orgasm pattern, and to accept and enjoy it rather than strive for the unrealistic goal of "perfect" orgasm performance. Develop your unique sexual voice and integrate orgasm into your couple sexual style. Your partner is your intimate, erotic friend, not your demanding critic. He is supportive and affirming rather than insisting you have a stereotypic, predictable orgasmic pattern. He accepts that in regularly orgasmic women, approximately 70% of encounters result in orgasm. Only 15% of women are orgasmic at each couple encounter.

REGULATING OUR EMOTIONAL AND SEXUAL DRIVES

We value sexuality more deeply by learning to regulate our emotional and sexual drives and arousal. We promote a healthy relationship with balanced emotional and sexual expression. The importance of cognitive-behavioral-emotional regulation is evident in couple relationship studies (e.g., Kirby, Baucom, & Peterman, 2007). Expressing negative emotions in an extreme way impairs emotional balance and your sexual environment. On the other hand, avoidance of feelings restricts emotional closeness and sexual passion.

Men's and women's bodies have "lust" (Buss, 1995), a "biological imperative" (Fisher, Aron, Mashek, & Brown, 2002), an "urge to merge" (Rolheiser, 1999). Healthy men and women accept and respect the power of their sexual urges. Men and women whose sexual behavior creates individual and relationship distress underestimate the importance of sex-drive regulation.

Sex-drive regulation is especially important for men because lust is not just a youthful stage but continues throughout life. Because the male sex drive is more specific and "object focused" than the female sex drive (Hamann, Herman, Nolan, & Walllen, 2004), men have a special responsibility to regulate and manage their sex drive wisely, just as they manage their desire for food, sleep, and exercise. This sex-drive regulation is cultivated through strategies such as carefully managing thoughts (Boul, 2007; McCarthy & Metz, 2008) and controlling impulses by limiting exposure to sex images and other enticements. When in an appropriate sexual situation, you can reverse the sexual regulation and freely engage in and enjoy heightened sex excitement.

Regulation requires both women and men to develop emotional sophistication. Emotions such as loneliness, anger, anxiety, resentment, or shame can be misunderstood as sexual feelings with an urge to assuage them by sex (Leeds, 2001) or, on the other extreme, used as a reason to disengage from sex. While tension reduction is a common and healthy use of sex, the unwitting sexualizing of nonsexual emotions fuels problematic behaviors such as making excessive demands on your partner, having affairs, or compulsively using pornography. Sexual health involves becoming aware and comfortable with negative emotions and healthy, nonsexual strategies to deal with them.

MEN AND LOW SEXUAL DESIRE

It is important to note that perhaps as many as 10% of men experience low desire for intimate couple sex (McCarthy & McDonald, 2009). The most common cause is a sexual secret such as a variant arousal pattern (e.g., fetish), preference for masturbatory sex rather than partner sex, a poorly processed history of a childhood sexual trauma, and conflict regarding sexual orientation. Acquired (secondary) sexual desire problems are much more common. The chief cause is sexual dysfunction, especially erectile dysfunction. The man has lost his confidence in achieving arousal and orgasm, and avoids couple sex because of embarrassment. Unresolved relationship conflict is also a common cause of inhibited sexual desire.

Promoting sexual desire involves mutually resolving chronic relationship conflicts, developing sexual self-confidence, and having a sex-positive attitude. Therapy can help address emotional or physical inhibitions, ensure realistic expectations about your body and emotions, and direct your attention to healthy sexual fantasy and erotic images.

Use of erotic fantasies is one of the most sensitive and controversial components of male (and female) sexuality. It is normal to have "abnormal" fantasies. Erotic fantasies can serve as a bridge to sexual desire, as well as a bridge to arousal and orgasm during couple sex. Two examples of the destructive use of fantasy is when the combination of secrecy, eroticism, and shame result in a compulsively controlling fantasy and when fantasy serves as a "wall" that creates disengagement from partner sex.

When a man's sex drive and a woman's emotional needs are well understood, respected, and managed, neither lust nor emotional distress subverts couple sexuality. You can freely enjoy sex. When over-regulated, these dynamics suppress sexual desire and cooperation. For the man, a poorly regulated sex drive can cause a variety of personal, sexual, and relationship problems such as compulsive sex and acting out sexually (Adams & Robinson, 2001). Conversely, a repressed sex drive deprives the man of pleasure and passion, causing personal and relational problems. For the woman, a poorly regulated emotional-sexual drive can lead her to pursue emotional connection yet avoid sexual activity, or to seek connection through an affair. Self-regulation of emotions and sex drive is not self-punishment or rebuke; it demonstrates self-respect and allows you to integrate physiological sexual drive, psychological well-being, and interpersonal cohesion into your couple sexual style.

ROBIN AND THAD

Robin, 63, was in a second marriage to Thad, aged 68. They'd been married 23 years. Robin had prided herself on being healthy and having a good body image. This was being tested by her recent diagnosis of breast cancer. Thad had a more erratic health history.

He'd been a smoker since age 14, although he successfully stopped at 45. However, he had continual problems with poor sleep habits (including taking 3-hour naps); very little exercise (his major exercise was walking stairs); and had poor eating habits (especially late-night snacks). He was 15 to 25 pounds above a healthy weight. Thad only drank socially, but he would overindulge on martinis two to three times a month.

Robin's oncologist believed in behavioral medicine, and the physician assistant counseled patients to adopt health habits as one component of cancer recovery. The physician assistant encouraged Robin to see cancer survivorship as a challenge to live life to the fullest, including marital sexuality. Robin asked for a couple consultation with Thad so he was better prepared to actively support her recovery.

The couple consultation was of great value to Robin and Thad. Robin accepted the necessity of breast surgery and a follow-up course of chemotherapy. During this process, she needed more, not less, comforting and sensual touch. She did not feel interested or ready for intercourse sex, but was open to being the giving partner, pleasuring Thad to orgasm on occasion. Thad was comfortable with manual stimulation, but wanted Robin to know that he preferred and valued interactive sex.

Robin preferred to sleep with Thad being present rather than having him stay downstairs watching TV. For this to be feasible, Thad needed to change his sleeping patterns, specifically go to bed earlier and limit naps to 30 to 45 minutes. Thad was surprised to discover that the changes in his sleep pattern dramatically improved the quality of his physical and psychological well-being. His increased energy had another positive side-effect, greater sexual desire. Robin welcomed a more physically, psychologically, and sexually engaged Thad.

A partner healing with cancer challenges the entire couple relationship. Illness causes people to feel anxious and out of control. An excellent couple technique is to focus on what you can control. Robin engaged in a walking and swimming program, and Thad agreed to be her exercise "buddy." Having an exercise partner or taking a class is motivating and keeps you accountable. The benefits were as great for Thad as for Robin. The same was true for establishing healthier cooking and eating patterns.

Couple sexuality can be a part of any illness recovery program. The challenge for Robin and Thad was to establish a new pleasuring/intercourse pattern that did not involve breast stimulation. This was actually easier for Robin than Thad because she found inner thigh, buttock, and kissing stimulation plus erotic fantasies built her arousal or "erotic flow" response more than breast stimulation. As is true of many couples, Thad was more aroused by giving breast stimulation than Robin enjoyed receiving it. Thad learned to "piggy-back" his arousal on Robin's arousal and to be open to her using a vaginal lubricant and guiding intromission. They felt like an intimate team in confronting the cancer and healing as a sexual couple.

VALUING YOUR SEXUAL BODY

Your body is meant to give and receive pleasure—not just your genitals but your whole body, from the top of your head to the soles of your feet. In valuing your body, you need not be a Hollywood star or spend a fortune at a spa. You do need to attend to your body in terms of exercise (don't be a couch potato), as well as hygiene (washing your face, genitals, and brushing your teeth). A good body image is not about "perfection" but about acceptance and a positive body presentation.

Body image is not primarily visual; body image is primarily about touch. The media "hype" portrays a perfect body image for single people under 25. What about people between 30 and 85 who are in partnered relationships? Especially real-life couples who will not make it into an R-rated video (which includes 99.5% of us). We all have a non-perfect body image Perfect body images are for videos and fantasies, not real life. Of course, you want a positive and accepting body image but that is not where your sexual desire or desirability lives. Sexual desire and desirability lie primarily in giving and receiving pleasure-oriented touch. Exercise 7.2 explores your body comfort.

We strongly believe in the value of non-demand pleasuring (affectionate, sensual, and playful touch). If made to choose between intercourse only and non-demand pleasuring only (a silly dichotomy because these are complementary dimensions), we would choose non-demand pleasuring as contributing more to intimacy and satisfaction. The essence of sexuality is sharing your body and feelings. Non-demand pleasuring has value in itself—to promote emotional and physical connection, facilitate intimacy, emphasize pleasure over performance, and, most important, promote a variable, flexible sexual repertoire that challenges the rigid performance roles that undermine sexual desire and satisfaction.

• • • • • • •

EXERCISE 7.2 VALUING YOUR SEXUAL BODIES

These psychosexual skill exercises make concepts of a bio-psychosocial approach to healthy sexuality personal and concrete. We ask you to do this exercise together, in the nude, and where you have access to both a full length mirror and a small, hand-held mirror. The focus is body awareness and acceptance by both you and your partner.

The person who feels more comfortable with his or her body begins. Contrary to "pop psych," this is usually the woman. She can stand facing the mirror, with her partner looking at her. What are your favorite non-genital body parts—your hair, eyes, fingers, thighs, feet, back? Choose two (not more) non-genital body parts that you feel are not attractive and note them for yourself and your partner. Genuine self-image and body acceptance involves being aware of both strengths and vulnerabilities.

Next, focus on your genitals—vulva, breasts, vagina, buttocks. This time, engage in light touching to increase your awareness (as well as your partner's) of positive sensations and sensual touch of genitals. If you are comfortable with this, use the small hand-held mirror to identify for yourself and your partner your clitoris, labia, and place a lubricated finger inside your vagina. Be aware of positive and negative intravaginal sensations. Remember, the focus is on comfort and awareness of your sexual body, not on proving anything to yourself or your partner.

Many women have mixed feelings about their breasts and breast touch. The joke for women is that breasts come in two sizes: too big and too small. Be aware of the most positive aspect of your breasts and demonstrate for your partner what type of breast touch feels most sensuous and you are most receptive to.

Then switch roles. The man faces the mirror and follows this format in identifying positive and two non-positive body parts. The special challenge for men is to not play to the extremes of braggadocio or the more common extreme of feeling that you are not the perfect man—focus on genuine body acceptance.

The second sensitive issue for men involves sensual touch of your penis and testicles. For most men, the only time you touch yourself genitally is a rapid, goal-oriented masturbation to orgasm. Slowing down the process and looking at your penis in an objective, accepting manner is not an easy task. You worry your penis is too small, too wrinkly, and not strong enough. Your penis is a positive, integral part of your sexual body. The more you accept yourself as a sexual man, the easier it is to share feelings and sensations with your partner. An important dimension is to accept your penis, both in its natural state (flaccid) as well as when erect. Men panic if their erection wanes. You might want to experiment with slow stroking (with or without sexual fantasies) so you become erect, then stop touching and be aware of your feelings and sensations as your erection goes down. Then resume sensual touch without performance pressure. Be confident that if you are relaxed and open, your erection will return. Many women find this a reassuring exercise because they learn that your penis is a natural part of your body, not a performance machine separate from the rest of you.

We suggest doing the next part of this exercise sitting up, in the nude, perhaps holding hands or putting your hand on your partner's cheek or heart. Speak directly about your vascular, neurological, and hormonal systems. Are there factors of illness, medication side-effects, aging, or poor health habits that interfere with the normal functioning of your sexual body? You are responsible for your health and sexual body. Be clear and specific about what you can do to promote sexual health. How can your partner be your supporter and ally in promoting a healthy body and sexual health?

NON-DEMAND PLEASURING

Non-demand pleasuring is a core strategy of GES and is integral to valuing variable, flexible couple sexuality. Ideally, each partner will be comfortable initiating a sensual, playful, erotic, or intercourse date. Use Exercise 7.3 to communicate to your partner what touch dimension is most inviting, as well as what you want and are open to. Remember: intimate coercion poisons pleasure and subverts couple sexuality. For example, during a given encounter, you might enjoy playful touch but not be open to erotic stimulation, while your partner had hoped to transition to intercourse but remains open to sensual and playful touch. Touching and sexuality are about pleasuring and communication. They are about requests, not demands. Then when you remove the prohibitions surrounding intercourse, you are opening new options for pleasuring, not creating an intercourse demand. Keep the focus on comfort, pleasure, sharing; do not fall into the trap of a performance orientation with either sexual demands or proscription.

• • • • • • •

EXERCISE 7.3 EXPLORING YOUR SEXUAL BODIES

In exploring your sexual body, we suggest a temporary prohibition on both intercourse and orgasm. Focus on greater awareness of your sexual body and your receptivity and responsivity to touch. We suggest taking turns (self-entrancement arousal) with a focus on comfort and sensations.

Since it is traditionally the man who begins sexual touching, we suggest the initial focus be on the man being aware of his body and receptivity to sensual pleasure. Begin by taking a shower or bath together, which establishes a comfortable milieu. The giving partner can experiment with sensual experiences (use of different sprays or bath oils, a body lotion, slow or playful touch, and body exploration rather than touch as a means to arousal). What are your favorite non-genital body parts to look at, touch, and explore? Touch for yourself rather than what you think he wants. He settles back, relaxes, takes in touch and sensations, and is not concerned about sexual response or performance. Focus on awareness. What body parts react most to touch, and what type of touch—manual, kissing, rubbing—feel the most sensuous? The notion that sexuality is integral to your whole body rather than limited to your penis and intercourse is a new experience for many men. Feelings are enhanced by kissing/licking his whole body, not just his lips or penis. This is new to most men. Non-demand pleasuring as a whole body experience adds a new dimension to sensuality and sexuality.

When it is time to switch roles with the woman as receiver, his focus is to view her as his intimate friend, not using "foreplay" to ready her for the main event of intercourse. Do touching and pleasuring for her, not trying to repeat your arousal pattern, second-guess her desires, or turn her on. She can focus on relaxing, exploring, and openness to touch all over her body, including non-perfect body parts. We suggest keeping your eyes closed so you can focus on sensations and your body's receptivity. What are your favorite body parts and touches? Remember: it is your body and your pleasure.

In ending this experience, we suggest holding each other, enjoying the closeness and warmth, and sharing perceptions and feelings. In the future, verbally and nonverbally guide your partner toward the body parts and types of touching you find most sensuous and pleasurable. For example, do you prefer mutual stimulation or taking turns? Multiple stimulation or single, focused stimulation? Does talking enhance intimacy, or does it distract from pleasure? Do you enjoy more or less kissing? Is playfulness more pleasurable than slow, rhythmic touching? How can you integrate awareness of your sexual body and non-demand pleasuring into your couple sexual style?

ENSURE YOUR PHYSICAL HEALTH FOR SEXUAL HEALTH

For lifelong sexual health, as well as positive sex attitudes and values, you need positive physical health habits such as physical conditioning, weight management, exercise, appropriate use of alcohol, and restful sleep patterns. Regular cardiovascular exercise, sensible diet and weight regimen, and adequate rest are crucial factors for sexual health in mid and later life. Remember that your body is the foundation for pleasure as well as sexual function.

Aging, Relaxation, and Sexual Response

The vitality of your vascular and neurological systems in youth can overcome high levels of anxiety and stress to allow you to be sexually functional. However, as you settle into your relationship and deal with jobs, parenting, household chores, and grow older, you need to treat your body and psychological milieu with more respect and care. Your youthful body is amazingly forgiving and resilient. As you age, your body becomes less forgiving.

An excellent example is stress and alcohol. Couples under 30 often work too hard, party too hard, drink too much, and argue too intensely, yet continue to be sexually functional. However, 10 years later you might be juggling two children, jobs, household responsibilities, stress, fatigue, or alcohol misuse, which interfere with sexual response. This makes sense biologically because stress, especially alcohol misuse, is a central nervous system depressant that interferes with vascular function. With the vitality of youth, the psychological association of sexuality and an alcohol high can overcome the negative neurovascular effect. But there comes a time when it no longer can.

One of the most empowering scientific findings is the viability and satisfaction that occurs with sex and aging. Healthy sex after 45 requires greater awareness of the biological, psychological, and relational factors that promote couple sex, and not engaging in physical, psychological, or relational behaviors that subvert healthy couple sexuality. This is why relaxation becomes more important as people and relationships mature. Be disciplined:

- Maintain healthy sleep habits.
- Quit smoking.
- Don't abuse alcohol or drugs (e.g., 1–2 drinks at the maximum).
- Follow good eating patterns.
- Exercise regularly.
- Address lingering or repetitious conflict (the importance of being a respectful, trusting, cooperative couple).
- Focus on maintaining a relaxed body during sex.
- Focus on mindfulness and pleasure.

As you age, you are more likely to adopt self-entrancement arousal techniques rather than rely on the youthful emphasis of partner interaction arousal. The focus of self-entrancement is relaxation and taking in sensations, usually using a giver-receiver format. This allows each partner to identify and request his or her unique "arousal continuum" and "erotic flow." This includes the type of initiation you are most receptive to, and the types and sequencing of touch that allow you to feel sensually and sexually responsive. Do you prefer single or multiple stimulation? How should you transition from non-genital to genital stimulation? What level of arousal is best for you in transitioning to intercourse?

SUMMARY

You have a right to feel proud of your body and sexuality. You do not need to have a perfect body or perfect sex in order to affirm your sexuality and the value of quality couple sex.

The biopsychosocial model is an excellent conceptual tool to increase awareness of the multi-causal, multi-dimensional factors that can contribute to or subvert individual and couple sexuality. You can adopt biological, psychological, and relational patterns that promote sexual health. Just as important, you need to confront problematic health, emotional, and relational patterns so they do not subvert your sexuality. You can promote efficient vascular, neurological, and hormonal function, and adjust to changes caused by illness, side-effects of medication, and physical aging. The really good news is that you can have a functional sexual body into your 80s. For that to occur, you need to adopt the variable, flexible GES model rather than cling to the traditional perfect intercourse performance approach. As your vascular and neurological systems become less efficient and resilient, you need each other more to actively share intimacy, pleasuring, and eroticism.

Do not fall into the self-fulfilling prophecy that "sex inevitably declines with age." While the sex that your youthful body relishes may mellow, the quality and delight that individuals and couples find can more than balance this physical moderation. Mature couples who practice GES would not trade youthful physical vibrancy for the psychological vibrancy and relationship quality of mature sexuality. Seasoned couples who pursue GES do a better job of integrating physical pleasures with the psychological and relationship joys that are a hallmark of deepening intimacy.

8

The Gender Team

Contrary to "pop psych," adult men and women in serious relationships are not so sexually different. Men are not from Mars and women are not from Venus, although they, of course, do have conflicts—often about sex. The topic of gender similarities and differences is very complex. Conflicts vary by the type and developmental phase of your relationship. Honor genuine gender differences and celebrate gender similarities. Don't be controlled by stereotypes or engage in the hyped gender wars promoted in the media and in bar room talk. We urge you to be wise in examining gender issues in your life and relationship. Focus on how these can enhance your couple sexual style.

In exploring gender issues, we use the biopsychosocial model. Our discussion is based on accurate and scientifically validated information involving biological, psychological, and social research. Knowledge is power. Understanding the complexity of gender differences and similarities allows you to make wise individual and relationship decisions that facilitate quality couple sexuality.

ACCEPTING DIFFERENCES AND VALUING YOUR INTIMATE RELATIONSHIP

The "ideal" belief was that each partner experienced the same intimate and erotic feelings at each encounter. This is the stuff of romantic movies, novels, and love songs. However, it is not the reality for the great majority of couples, nor should it be. It is normal and healthy to have different experiences of intimacy and eroticism, even during a specific sexual encounter. Enjoy the lively variability and flexibility of healthy couple sexuality. Revel in this rather than worry or argue about it. You are sexual people; you are not mechanical performance machines or actors in a romantic comedy. Quality sexuality is about developing your couple sexual style that balances intimacy and eroticism in your own special way.

COMMON SEXUAL DIFFERENCES

Couples differ regarding sexual features such as frequency, behaviors and styles, erotic or romantic words, invitation versus seduction, and a focus on emotional feelings or physical pleasures. Those couples who work as a team do well, while couples who allow these differences to create conflict are vulnerable to sexual power struggles and intense dissatisfaction.

Certainly, there are significant gender differences in brain function, genitals, hormonal function, and vascular and neurological systems. These differences continue throughout adulthood, but become less defined and controlling with the aging of your bodies and especially the maturity of your relationship. Accurate knowledge of how your body functions, as well as how your partner's body functions, is crucial to quality couple sexuality. Poor health habits, misunderstandings, illness, side-effects of medications, and unrealistic expectations regarding your own or your partner's body cause disappointment, frustration, and sexual dysfunction.

> **Physiologically, male and female bodies are both similar and different.**

Physiologically, male and female bodies are both similar and different. On talk shows, sexual differences between women and men are portrayed as very simple and clear-cut.

In reality, they are quite complex. Sexual physiology is multi-causal and multi-dimensional. Psychologically healthy women and men appreciate the complexity, respect it, and recognize and enjoy the differences while acknowledging and valuing similarities of being a male or female and a sexual couple.

PHYSIOLOGICAL DIFFERENCES BETWEEN THE SEXES

Understanding your sexual body and sexual physiology enhances your acceptance of your partner. The physiological function of the genitals is similar for men and women, although hormonal factors and sexual socialization differs. For example, the erogenous zones (neural pathways involving sexual pleasure) of the man—including his penis and testicles—are similar to the woman's clitoris and vulva. The breasts and nipples of both men and women can be sensual and erotic, although sexual socialization has focused much more on the sexual response of the female breast.

Male genitals, specifically the penis, stand out very prominently. Your biological arousal is easily signaled by your erection, which is a sign of healthy physiological function. Erection occurs when the penis responds to sexual pleasure by engorging with blood. Each night when you are asleep, whether sexually active or not, you typically have a 10- to 20-minute erection approximately every 60 to 90 minutes, ranging from 3 to 5 erections per night. Physiologically, nighttime erections are a way for your sexual body to oxygenate the tissues of your penis and maintain healthy function.

The woman's clitoris has traditionally been viewed as more "mysterious" by both women and men. It is a smaller organ than the penis, and thus the nerve endings are more densely packed. Similar to the penis, each night when you are asleep, whether sexually active or not, you also have 10- to 20-minute swellings of your clitoris several times per night to maintain healthy function. Unlike the penis, which also has the function of urination, the sole function of your clitoris is sexual pleasure. While the penis is easily observable, especially in the erect state, the clitoris typically retracts under the clitoral hood, responds to indirect stimulation of the clitoral shaft (direct stimulation can be painful), and is less a symbol of arousal. During intercourse, your clitoris is indirectly stimulated during thrusting. Physiologically, female sexual function is more complex and variable than male sexual function.

HOW YOUR SEXUAL BODY "WORKS"

Understanding your sexual body (and your partner's) will improve sexual self-confidence and help you develop positive, realistic sexual expectations. This includes accepting the role and function of your vascular, neurological, and hormonal systems. For both women and men, sex response is primarily a vascular function. The man's pelvic area, including testicles, engorges with blood to make the penis larger and firmer. Increased blood flow to a woman's genitals enhances vaginal lubrication, clitoral enlargement, breast swelling, and vaginal changes that facilitate penile entry and intercourse. Your neurological system responds to both mental and physical stimulation to enhance the sexual response process. Your hormonal system provides the physiological underpinning for sexual desire and function.

The basic guideline is that whatever is good for your physical body will be good for your sexual body. Likewise, what is harmful for your physical body is harmful for your sexual body. Thus, in terms of physical health and health habits, you want to promote vascular, neurological, and hormonal function. With aging, but especially illness and unwanted side-effects of medications, you need to be aware of factors subverting vascular, neurological, and hormonal function and how to compensate for these.

The sexual ideal is that both partners are physically healthy; maintain healthy sleep, exercise, and eating patterns; do not smoke and do moderate or no drinking; and take no medications other than

What is good for your physical body is good for your sexual body.

vitamins. Unfortunately, that is not the reality for most couples. However, you want to be as healthy as possible and to positively influence your partner to adopt healthy behavioral habits.

Primary prevention of sexual problems involves being as aware, knowledgeable, and healthy as possible. Secondary prevention involves being aware of normal bodily and sexual changes with illness and aging, and using your medical, psychological, relational, and psychosexual skill resources to maintain the highest level of sexual function possible. A valuable preventative resource is to schedule a sexual health consultation as a couple with your internist or family physician.

When dealing with a medical problem—whether heart disease, cancer, diabetes, stroke, multiple sclerosis, or bipolar disorder—you want to be an active, informed patient. Adopt health habits that facilitate physical function, and change habits that undermine your body. In addition, be sure to understand medication side-effects and discuss changing medications, reducing unwanted side-effects, or how to compensate for them. Your physician wants to be helpful but might not be comfortable or skilled in dealing with sexual problems. Letting him/her know that you are not asking for sex counseling but how to be an active, involved patient without sacrificing sexual function invites your physician to give you essential information with a focus on biological/medical factors that do not unnecessarily limit couple sexuality. You can savor and reinforce quality couple sexuality in illness and health from your 20s to your 80s.

SONIA AND KARL

Sonia is a 58-year-old woman in a second marriage of 29 years with 56-year-old Karl. This is his first marriage. Fifteen years previously, Sonia had been diagnosed with multiple sclerosis (MS). She has regular appointments with her neurologist and intermittent physical therapy. Karl has moderate, chronic medical problems of high blood pressure and high cholesterol, plus chronic back pain. He is taking blood pressure and cholesterol medications prescribed by his internist, as well as seeing a chiropractor on an intermittent basis for the back pain. Sonia and Karl were supportive of each other's medical problems, but neither was a knowledgeable, active patient.

When Sonia's neurologist retired, a friend Sonia met through an online MS support group highly recommended a younger, behavioral medicine-oriented neurologist. Sonia really likes his integrative, activist approach to managing MS, and she was motivated to be a knowledgeable, active MS patient. He was the first physician who ever asked her about sexual desire and function. He did not want to provide sex therapy but was an approachable physician who wanted to be of help. In fact, Sonia and Karl had fallen into the trap of a nonsexual marriage (being sexual less than 10 times a year). Sonia felt it was caused by Karl not finding her sexually attractive because of the MS or that his pain and blood pressure problems made him sexually less functional. They had never discussed this. They felt embarrassed and treated sex issues with benign neglect.

The neurologist offered to see them for one conjoint session to discuss their medical conditions and how these could affect their sexual bodies and physiological function. Sonia was enthusiastic. Although Karl was a bit intimidated, he agreed to join her. The doctor emphasized the importance of being active, involved patients. He said that although their diseases and medications did alter sexual response, they did not control sexual response. If Sonia and Karl were interested. he would be glad to provide a referral to a couple sex therapist who specialized in a behavioral medicine approach to illness and sexuality. Karl did not know that such a specialty even existed, and they accepted the referral.

The physician then explained how each of their illnesses (and the medications to treat them) impacted their vascular and neurological systems. There was minimal impact hormonally. MS is a neurological disease that cannot be cured, but it can be managed. Sonia's MS was in the mild-to-moderate range, and the physician wanted to treat symptoms more aggressively. He urged Sonia to be an active patient, especially in terms of the health habits of adequate sleep and regular exercise. He encouraged Karl to be Sonia's "exercise buddy." They agreed to reinforce each other in improving sleep patterns, including going to bed before 10:30 and limiting naps to one 45-minute nap in the early afternoon. Karl was urged to talk to his internist about taking a proactive approach to eating and exercising, and taking his blood pressure on a weekly basis. The physician also counseled Sonia and Karl that sex was a good and inexpensive form of exercise.

The couple sex therapist helped Sonia and Karl accept that sexuality could be an integral part of their lives and marriage. They would need to be intimate, erotic friends and to cooperate as an intimate team. The joy of sex after 50, especially when there are medical problems, is the man and woman need each other in a way they didn't in their 20s and 30s. This is both more challenging and more rewarding. Psychological, relational, and psychosexual skill factors are important in compensating for less efficient vascular and neurological systems caused by illness, side-effects of medications, and aging. In terms of specifics, sexual encounters needed to be semi-planned when Sonia was feeling energetic and her body was more flexible. This meant having sex in the late morning or early afternoon after Sonia took her medications and after water aerobics. Karl adopted the GES approach to erections and intercourse. Specifically, this meant using the psychosexual skills of multiple stimulation, transitioning to intercourse at high levels of erotic flow, and being comfortable transitioning to mutual erotic, non-intercourse sex when sex did not transition naturally into intercourse.

These were daunting changes for Karl. However, with the new knowledge of physiological, psychological and sexual realities, guidance from the sex therapist, and especially Sonia's enthusiasm, Karl gained comfort and confidence with a variable, flexible approach to couple sexuality. The challenge for Karl, as it is for the majority of men, was to give up the tyranny of the perfect intercourse performance and replace it with the variable, flexible GES model. Karl learned that this was first-class male and couple sexuality, not about his being a second-class man who had to "settle." Most helpful was the clinician commenting that Karl was being a "wise" man who would enjoy couple sexuality into his 80s.

Our refrain of desire, sensuality, pleasuring, and satisfaction reaches fruition with couples after 50, especially those dealing with lessened biological efficacy caused by illness and side-effects of medications. Even more important is to play to your strengths as sexual partners. This includes the woman enjoying her new role as the active sexual friend whose partner needs her. Sonia told Karl that she liked his "grown-up erections" more than his youthful "show-up erections." Just as important, Karl learned to "piggy-back" his arousal on Sonia's arousal. Besides revitalizing their sexual relationship, Sonia and Karl's revamped approach to intimacy led to a better quality and more satisfying couple sexuality than when they were younger.

BLENDING GENDER DIFFERENCES IN QUALITY COUPLE SEXUALITY

Respectfully accepting gender differences and valuing gender similarities contributes immeasurably to desire, pleasure, and satisfaction. The traditional sex goal for men was orgasm, and for women intimate connection. Gender differences in sexual purpose and arousal are most clearly observed in teenagers and young adults. With experience and with maturing of the relationship, these traditional gender roles become more flexible and complementary. However, even in adult couples, biological differences are still apparent, especially the man's more rapid sexual response and the clear signal of arousal—his erection.

Ease and rapidity of desire and arousal is greater for men, who tend to see the pleasuring process as being for the woman, not for them. This is understandable, but very unwise. Placing value on giving and receiving pleasurable touch is the foundation of enduring desire and quality couple sexuality. Men can grow to enjoy and value pleasure, even though in their younger years they didn't need it. A pleasure-orientation will thwart sexual dysfunction with mid-life and growing older. Even more important, it affirms you as an intimate team that celebrates pleasuring and sexuality.

The concept of pleasuring is more inviting and inherent to female sexual response. The great majority of women learn sexual response as an intimate, interactive process and value this rather than autonomous sex. Even more important, pleasuring allows partners to become aware that couple sexuality is inherently variable and flexible, which facilitates accepting the GES model rather than the perfect intercourse performance model. The idea is to regard sexual pleasure as including sensual, playful, and erotic touch, with intercourse as the natural continuation of the pleasuring/erotic flow process, not a pass-fail test separate from pleasuring.

Psychologically, one difference is that men are more likely to use sex as a tension reducer, and women are more likely to use sex as a means to express, maintain, and deepen emotional connection. As couples mature, the hope is that the man will value intimacy and non-demand pleasuring, and that the woman will develop a sexual voice that includes using sex as a tension reducer, expansion of physical pleasures, and a means to reestablish connection after life's distractions, conflict, or alienation.

Relationally, biological vigor, and traditional roles lead men to initiate and emphasize intercourse frequency, while women emphasize affection and non-demand pleasuring. With maturity, gender differences begin to blur, and similarities and complementary roles are emphasized.

Perhaps gender differences and challenges are greatest in the area of psychosexual skills. Frankly, the GES model and adopting a variable, flexible approach is much more of a challenge for the man than the woman. Her challenge is to develop a strong, resilient sexual voice and to integrate and value regular erotic strategies and techniques into her sexual style. The man, as her erotic friend, is of great value in reinforcing this growth. He accepts that her feelings and preferences will be different than his. Again, the issue is being complementary and honoring diversity, avoiding the "my-way-versus-your-way" power struggle.

The challenge for the man is to enthusiastically embrace variable, flexible couple sexuality and to understand that the GES model involves first-class sexuality. This requires a conscious change from the cultural notion that defines virility in terms of penis size, autonomous erections, intercourse as a pass-fail test, orgasm as mandatory, and genital stimulation as unnecessary to facilitate erotic flow. Human sexuality, including male sexuality, is multi-causal, multi-dimensional, and complex—with a respect for individual, couple, cultural, and value differences.

THE CLASSIC MODEL FOR HUMAN SEXUAL RESPONSE

For many years, the classic human sexual response cycle (Masters & Johnson, 1970; Kaplan, 1974) described the physiological and psychological sex response pattern in terms of desire, arousal (excitement), plateau, orgasm, and resolution (satisfaction). Sexual dysfunctions are difficulties with one or several of these functional stages. For example, chronic absence of sexual interest was a deficit in desire; erectile dysfunction and inhibited female excitement were deficits in arousal; and premature ejaculation and delayed orgasm were orgasm disorders.

BASSON MODEL OF RESPONSIVE SEX DESIRE AND AROUSAL

While the assumption that male and female responsivity are similar may still be accurate physiologically, it has become apparent that sexual desire for men is more physiologically driven and for women more psychologically responsive. The major sex therapy concept in the past decade has been that of "responsive female

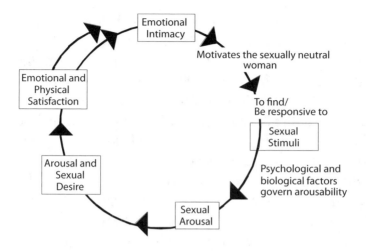

Figure 8.1 Responsive sexual desire process.

sexual desire," (Basson, 2007), in which sexual fantasies and need for orgasm are not the sexual drivers. Female sexual desire is more often a responsive, interactive process rather than a spontaneous, autonomous experience (Figure 8.1).

There are two components to heightening female sexual desire. The first involves positive emotions and non-demand pleasuring. Her sexual desire develops after physical and emotional connection. Second, the woman and her partner understand that there is a range of pleasure dimensions and choices rather than just a demand for intercourse and orgasm. Quality couple sexuality lives in pleasure and choice. Performance pressures and partner demand poison sexual desire.

Healthy female desire and response involves awareness of sexual anticipation, emotional benefits, and openness and receptivity to touch. Her responsive sexual desire is based on intimacy, comfort and security with her partner, cooperative interaction, pleasure, and variability/flexibility. It is important for partners to realize that it is common for desire to ebb and flow without worrying that this signals a problem. Desire is part of variability unless inhibited desire becomes a chronic pattern.

When couples stop being sexual—whether at 30, 50, or 70—it is almost always the man's decision, made unilaterally, conveyed nonverbally, and controlled by avoidance. He clings to the traditional male model of total predictability and sexual performance as a pass-fail test. However, in a committed relationship over time, male sexual desire is also "responsive," a very valuable concept for most men, especially by their 50s, if not before.

Young adult men learn sexuality as easy, highly predictable, and autonomous. Sex feels like a biologically driven need for gender affirmation, intercourse, and orgasm. Enjoy that phase of your individual and couple sexuality. But it is the wise sexual man who is open to variable, flexible GES. The growth goals of GES promote gender respect and cooperation as an intimate team and ensure enduring desire (see Exercise 8.1).

• • • • • • •

EXERCISE 8.1   BEING INTIMATE AND EROTIC FRIENDS

You value a quality sexual relationship when you comfortably share your physical bodies, psychological preferences, and feelings; cooperate as intimate and erotic friends; and adopt functional psychosexual skills. "Gender wars" might occur in the sociopolitical arena, but should not enter into your couple relationship.

This writing-and-talking exercise asks you to make personal and concrete the biopsychosocial model. Leave stereotypes and being "politically correct" outside your relationship. Rather, implement what is true for you as individuals and as a couple, and discuss how you can translate this to promote quality couple sexuality.

No matter your age, pinpoint ways in which your physiological sexual responses are similar and in what ways they are different. Biologically, what drives sexual desire for each of you? What facilitates your healthy sexual body and what subverts your sexual body (vascular, hormonal, neurological)? How can you play to your similarities and utilize your unique biological strengths to facilitate healthy couple sexuality?

Psychologically, are each of you willing to accept the challenge of valuing your sexual similarities and respectfully managing differences in a manner that enhances sexual satisfaction? Clearly state your sexual preferences and feelings. Just as clearly, be assertive about what you do or your partner does to subvert healthy sexuality. What are your psychological requests to make couple sex more comfortable and functional?

Relationally, do you see yourselves as both intimate and erotic friends? If so, you have a major relationship resource. If not, what is each of you willing to do to promote couple sexual cooperation and what can you request of your partner? Sex is an intimate team sport. Satisfaction and bonding constitute the ultimate goal of sexuality.

Psychosexual skills (e.g., pelvic muscle use, arousal styles, kinds of touch, erotic flow, flexibility) are often ignored yet crucially important in promoting quality couple sexuality. The way you learned to be sexual as a single person in your 20s will not serve you well in a serious relationship. Each of you should choose at least one and up to three psychosexual skills involving desire, arousal, intercourse, orgasm, or afterplay to adopt in your relationship. Talk with your partner so that he or she can be your ally and supporter in implementing these psychosexual skills. Remember, the focus of this exercise is to utilize the biopsychosocial model and use all your resources to be a comfortable, functional gender-intimacy team.

GENDER AND POSITIVE, REALISTIC SEXUAL EXPECTATIONS

Knowledge is power—and the opposite of simplistic stereotypes. Basing your sexual expectations on accurate biological, psychological, and social information regarding gender similarities and differences is essential for enjoying and valuing quality couple sexuality. Value complexity, respect individual differences, and emphasize what is comfortable and functional for you and your partner. Appreciating gender complexity and accepting differences helps couples cooperate and deepen their feeling as an intimate team.

Positive, realistic sexual expectations emphasize the evolving dimensions of biological, psychological, and social factors, especially with your growing older and the maturity of your relationship. Biologically, for couples in their 60s and older, both the man's and woman's vascular and neurological systems remain functional, although less efficient and resilient. Desire, pleasure, and satisfaction flourish, especially if each partner views the maturing process as an opportunity to turn toward each other, to encourage intimate, erotic response, and to adopt varying means to achieve it. Acting as an intimate, erotic team with positive expectations enhances sexuality for both partners.

SUMMARY

Simplistic gender wars make for great talk show and bar arguments, but subvert psychological, relational, and sexual health for real-life couples. The bottom line is that men and women who value quality couple sexuality are able to enjoy and integrate gender understandings into a comfortable, functional couple sexual style. Enjoy similarities, and accept and accommodate differences so your diverse capabilities, feelings, and preferences complement one another. As you and your relationship mature, psychological and relational similarities outnumber differences, which dissolve and are replaced by an appreciation of gender similarities in valuing desire, pleasure, eroticism, and satisfaction. Variable, flexible couple sexuality and acting as intimate allies in adopting the GES approach set the foundation for both partners to savor lifelong sexual health and satisfaction.

9

Sexual Pleasure and Function

Although the idea is counter-intuitive, relaxation is the foundation of sexual pleasure, function, and satisfaction. By relaxation, we do not mean unen-

Relaxation is the launch pad for arousal and erotic flow.

thusiastic or lethargic interactions, but calm pleasures. The psychological importance of relaxation for both women and men is that it enhances responsivity to touch, which is at the core of sexual arousal. The goal of relaxation is body comfort, simple openness to touch, and enhanced sexual pleasure.

Relaxation is the opposite of anxiety and a performance agenda. Anxiety subverts sexual response. All three dimensions of relaxation are important—physical relaxation, psychological comfort, and feeling open, desired, and accepted as a couple. While they do not directly result in arousal and orgasm, relaxation and sensuality set the stage for sexual response. Without a basic sense of comfort, relaxation, and sensual touch, your attempts at eroticism are on very shaky ground unless you're a young person in your 20s. The vitality of youth can overcome high levels of anxiety, tension, and performance anxiety that otherwise inhibits physical function.

Relaxation becomes increasingly important after age 30. The foundational work of Masters and Johnson (1970) and the behavioral exercises they developed ("sensate focus") were grounded on biophysiologic relaxation as the cornerstone of sexual function.

> The "erotic flow" of sexual response is: relaxation→pleasure→arousal→eroticism→ intercourse→orgasm

Masters and Johnson advocated that by removing the barriers to healthy sexual function (for example, performance anxiety, shame, cognitive distraction, relationship conflict) and by promoting physical, emotional, and interpersonal relaxation, your body and mind would "naturally" respond and experience arousal and orgasm.

The abundant evidence of the role of anxiety in sexual dysfunction (Barlow, 1988) points to the need for physiologic and psychologic relaxation to ameliorate performance pressure and anxiety. The importance of the role of relaxation for pleasure and function is difficult for men to appreciate. They especially fear that relaxation will result in routine sex and boredom. Men worry that physiologic relaxation during sexual touch could cause an erection problem because of reduced erotic stimulation. This misconstrues the positive role of relaxation in sexual response. Being relaxed and receptive to touch and sensations naturally results in achieving arousal. In fact, physical relaxation and the focus on pleasure facilitates "easy and reliable" erections (Metz & McCarthy, 2004). The mechanism of the pro-erection medications (Viagra, Levitra, Cialis) demonstrates that physiological relaxation facilitates erection. Pro-erection medications relax the musculature surrounding the arteries in the penis to enable blood flow and erection. Since sexual response for both women and men is primarily a vascular process (blood flow to your genitals), sexual feelings are enhanced, especially when you utilize self-entrancement arousal (described in detail in Chapter 10).

Physiologic relaxation is the vital mechanism of erection for the man and arousal for the woman. Partners would do well to relax both mind and body during sexual pleasuring. Striving for perfection undermines physiologic and psychological relaxation, and in turn produces performance pressure and anxiety. This is why it is counterproductive for a man to pressure himself to achieve perfect sexual performance. In fact, it is important for him and his partner not to work too hard sexually.

VISUALIZING RELAXATION

The relaxation/arousal sequence can be conceptualized as a process of relaxation, comfort, sensual touch, playful touch, arousal, erotic flow, orgasm. If you think of this process as being on a 10-point scale of pleasure from 0 (neutral) to 10 (orgasm), relaxation centers you from 1 to 3 on the pleasure scale. Sensuality will not produce an orgasm, but sensuality does lay the receptivity/responsivity foundation for subjective and objective arousal. Sexual arousal involves a congruence of subjective (erotic turn-on) and objective (neurovascular) response. The subjective underpinning of relaxation involves letting go of feelings of stress and tension and replacing them with a sense of calm, openness and closeness. Objectively, relaxation involves reaching a physical state of warmth and heaviness (or for some, floating lightness), and savoring feelings of physical comfort. The key is to start with increased awareness of your entire body (Exercise 9.1). Like any other bodily skill, practice increases your comfort and confidence.

• • • • • • •

EXERCISE 9.1 TOTAL BODY PHYSICAL RELAXATION

This is a combined individual and couple exercise. We ask you to increase awareness of your physical body and reinforce each other as you learn to be "master relaxers."

You can do this on your own or you can purchase a commercial relaxation/guided imagery CD. If you choose the latter, be sure it's a skill-based tape (with instructions to identify muscle groups and relax them) rather than just a "good feelings" tape. Identify muscle groups by first tensing them and then letting go and relaxing.

We suggest you begin by taking in a long, slow deep breath with the self-instruction of "relax" as you breathe in and "calm" as you breathe out. Slow, rhythmic breathing is the most powerful technique in relaxation and can be reinforced throughout the relaxation session as well as random times during the week.

We suggest relaxing one muscle group at a time—tensing for 5 to 10 seconds, and then letting go and relaxing. Notice the difference between feelings of pressure/tension/anxiety and the warm, comfortable feelings of relaxation. Relax each muscle group for 45 to 60 seconds. Notice the contrast between anxiety / pressure / concern and feelings of calm / comfort / acceptance. At each practice, notice the physical and psychological differences, letting go more and more and deeper and deeper. Relaxation is both a skill and an art. With continued practice you can become master relaxers.

Here are some suggested physical exercises:

1. *Make a fist with both hands—be aware of sensations in your fingers, hands, and forearms.*
2. *Press your forearms on the chair and feel the tensions in the upper part of your arms.*
3. *Tense your forehead by frowning hard.*
4. *Keeping your eyes closed, pretend you are staring at a spot in the middle of your forehead.*
5. *Press your tongue against the roof of your mouth and feel the tensions in your mouth and throat.*
6. *Pull the muscles of your mouth back, and feel the tension in your mouth and cheeks.*
7. *Move your neck to the front, back, sides and feel the stress and tensions in your neck muscles.*
8. *Focus on the tension in your upper back by hunching your shoulders back and up.*
9. *Tense the muscles in your lower back by arching your back as far as you can.*

10. *Tense your chest muscles by rotating your shoulders forward as if they could touch each other.*
11. *Tense your stomach muscles by pushing them in as far as they can go.*
12. *Raise up your pelvis and tighten the anal sphincter muscle, feel the tension in your pelvis and buttocks.*
13. *Press your heels on the floor and feel the tension in your legs and thighs.*
14. *Lift your feet 2 inches off the floor and feel the tension in your legs.*
15. *Point your toes toward your face and feel the tension in your legs and calves.*
16. *Curl your toes under as if you were burying them in the sand and feel the tension in your toes and feet.*

As you continue to use your breathing and relax, be aware of where in your body you feel the most relaxed. Savor and deepen those feelings. To enhance relaxation, focus on an imagery scene that for you is associated with physical and psychological relaxation such as lying on the beach listening to the waves and feeling the sun on your body or walking in the woods feeling the coolness, beauty, and silence of the forest.

You can share enjoyment of physical relaxation and awareness of your body's comfort and receptivity. The base of sensuality is touch, which builds on the foundation of relaxation and adds pleasurable dimensions. Comfort and confidence with relaxation is an excellent sexual resource.

THE RELAXATION SHORTCUT: YOUR PELVIC MUSCLES (PM)

The shortcut to establish sufficient physical relaxation for sexual function is to relax your pelvic muscles, the pubococcygeal or "PM" muscles. For women, PM relaxation is equivalent to Kegel exercises, which are practiced for childbirth, as well as sexual response. For men, it means learning to identify and relax the pelvic floor muscles. A way to identify the PM is to stop urination mid-stream. The muscles you use are your pelvic muscles. You can learn to relax pelvic muscles by using a tense-relax procedure. Some people repeat this movement 5 to 10 times daily, others 10 to 25 times.

HOW DO I KNOW IF I AM RELAXED ENOUGH FOR GREAT SEX?

You've heard of the term "tight ass"? With stress and tension, it is common for our muscles to tense up, which inevitably means you tighten your PM. When your PM is tight, the rest of your body tends to follow. So for quality sex, don't be a "tight ass." Relax your pelvic muscles for greater pleasure and easier sexual function. Exercise 9.2 demonstrates how.

• • • • • • •

EXERCISE 9.2 PELVIC MUSCLE EXERCISE FOR THE MAN AND WOMAN

Each day, take a minute (60 seconds) to:

1. *Tighten and hold your pelvic muscles and consciously focus on the sensation for 3 seconds.*
2. *Then relax the pelvic muscles for 3 seconds, keeping your attention focused on the calm sensations.*

Do this tightening and relaxing 10 times (3 seconds tight, 3 seconds calm), keeping your attention on comfortable physical sensations throughout this 1-minute exercise.

MINDFUL RELAXATION

Another relaxation technique focuses on the use of cognition and imagery to enhance feelings of relaxation. There is an increasing professional and public literature about "mindfulness," which focuses on mental relaxation and acceptance. There are many techniques and variations on the theme of mindfulness that you can incorporate into your individual and couple sensuality to enhance relaxation. The following case history is a prime example of this technique.

SYLVIA AND DAMON

Sylvia, aged 32, and Damon, 31, were in a 3-year relationship and had been living together for over 2 years. Sylvia had been divorced after 2 years of marriage and had a 7-year old son. Damon was divorced after 3 years of marriage and had no children. There was a solid connection and commitment between Sylvia and Damon, although neither was interested in having another child or in a marital commitment. Their sexual relationship had been high intensity and frequent in the first few months.

They were a sexually functional couple, but with infrequent sex (being sexual less than 25 times a year) about twice a month. Between work, parenting Sylvia's son, household chores, and community activities, they didn't feel energetic enough to devote time to sex. Intercourse and orgasm weren't compelling enough to be a priority. For them, sex was a big performance. Since it was a major investment of energy unless both were really interested, they skipped sex. The result was a low intercourse frequency, as well as low frequency of other types of sensual and sexual touching. Research estimates are that the average number of intercourse experiences per year is 61. For Sylvia and Damon, it was much lower.

It was Damon who attended a workplace stress management program that included teaching physical relaxation as well as a class on mindfulness. These were new and intriguing concepts for Damon, and during the week he practiced them at home. Sylvia also expressed interest. At the second and final session, the trainer mentioned that the many uses of relaxation and mindfulness included enhancing sexual pleasure. This really intrigued Damon, and Sylvia was even more interested in this application.

Damon suggested that they lie on the floor of the family room and spend 20 minutes practicing relaxation, including guided imagery of a relaxation scene. They used a tape provided in the training class. Both found this relaxing and enjoyable. Three days later, Sylvia suggested they take the relaxation concept a step further, again in the family room. She put on a jazz CD and gave Damon a non-genital body massage—his whole body, not just his back. The combination of massage and relaxation was very powerful in teaching Damon to value sensual touch for itself. It was also important for Damon to learn to give sensual touch. Damon previously thought of touch as "foreplay." He would quickly switch to genital stimulation to ready Sylvia for intercourse. Sylvia was a proponent of non-demand pleasuring, which could extend for 15–20 minutes, but this had dropped out of her repertoire. Their experience with relaxation and massage reinforced that her desire and sexual response was much enhanced if it was based on comfort and non-demand pleasuring.

After these initial experiences, Sylvia and Damon talked about the role of relaxation and touch in their sexual desire and couple sexual style. Their most important insight was the concept of a variable, flexible approach to relaxation and pleasure (rather than sex as a major intercourse performance), which made couple sexuality much more inviting. Relaxation, non-demand pleasuring, and intercourse were different dimensions of touch and extended their sexual pleasure. Damon and Sylvia now had a valuable relational resource based on relaxation, mindfulness, and touch, which energized their relationship both in terms of quality and frequency (McCarthy & McCarthy, 2002).

THE BUFFET OF TOUCH AND PLEASURE

With relaxation, sensuality can flourish, allowing you to soak up physical pleasure purely for itself. This is not as easy as it sounds. Pressure for sexual performance (e.g., "sex on demand") is a common and toxic feature of distressed sexual experience. For example, as many as four of five couples who follow infertility protocols with their "demand" for intercourse determined by the woman's temperature (ovulation), experience erectile dysfunction and/or inhibited sexual desire (Burns, 2006). The infertility protocol unintentionally sets up performance anxiety (a common cause of sexual dysfunction) and undermines pleasure. In the GES approach, sensual awareness, touch, and pleasure are emphasized along with function.

Sexual desire, arousal, and erotic flow are easy and tangible when you value and enjoy touch. An empowering concept is the five dimensions of touch: affection/comfort, sensual, playful, erotic, and intercourse. The GES model encourages you to value at least three and ideally all five dimensions of touch and pleasure (Figure 9.1).

Each type of touch expands into the next when you take advantage of the opportunities to foster your sexual response and erotic flow. At the same time, each component is valuable for itself as a form of sharing pleasure rather than just "foreplay" for "real

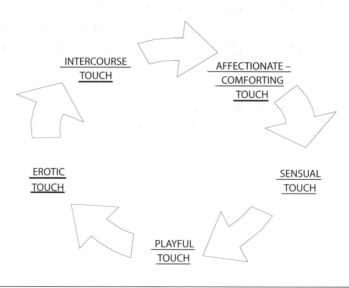

Figure 9.1 The five dimensions of touch.

sex" (intercourse). Without a pleasure orientation, quality couple sexuality suffers.

To illustrate this, think of pleasure on a 10-point scale of intensity, with 1 being affection/comfort and 10 being orgasm:

1. *Affectionate/comforting touch* refers to the range of non-sexual touch. Affectionate touch occurs in day-to-day closeness that indicates caring and fondness. It includes warm embraces, holding hands to reinforce feelings of intimacy, clothes-on kissing, and hugging to congratulate and celebrate. Comforting touch occurs during exceptional times of stress or challenge such as a work crisis, illness, major disappointments, a parenting emergency, or death in the family. Comfort touch is an important physical connection that usually takes place outside the bedroom and "tenderizes," soothes, and enhances your relationship. Comforting touch provides the safe harbor in life. Comforting and affectionate touches are not sexual, although each is essential to a cohesive, bonding climate that can facilitate sexual interest and receptivity. These kinds of touch promote essential feelings in your relationship environment of physical comfort in which your sensual and erotic life thrives (see Chapter 6). On our pleasure scale, affection/comfort touch anchors pleasure at 1. The other four dimensions involve sensual/sexual touch.

2. *Sensual touch* includes non-genital holding, stroking, cuddling, and massage. Sensual touch involves receptivity and responsivity and is the start of the sexual process. On our 10-point scale, sensuality is 2–3.

3. *Playful touch* intermixes non-genital and genital touch and can include whole body massage, romantic or erotic dancing, showering or bathing together, fun or seductive touch, and sexual playfulness. On our pleasure scale, playful touch is 4–6.

4. *Erotic, non-intercourse touch* involves manual, oral, rubbing, or vibrator stimulation and sometimes taking emotional and sexual risks ("stretching"). Levels of pleasure can be from 7–10 (orgasm). Some people really enjoy the erotic flow to orgasm, while others strongly prefer being orgasmic during intercourse.

5. *Intercourse* is the fifth dimension of pleasure. Both conceptually and in terms of technique, intercourse is best understood as a natural continuation of the pleasure/erotic flow process. You risk problems when you set up intercourse as a pass-fail test apart from the pleasuring process. Young couples learn to switch to intercourse as soon as they can (at levels 4 or 5 of pleasure), based on whether the male has an erection and the woman is beginning lubrication. A very important psychosexual skill is to learn to transition to intercourse at high levels of arousal: 7 or 8 on the 10-point scale.

Each dimension of touch has value as a way to experience pleasure. Many couples fall into the trap of intercourse or nothing. In other words, if touching is more than comfort/affection, the demand is to continue to intercourse.

> **Valuing each type of touch is a solid base for quality couple sexuality.**

So if you are not interested in intercourse, you don't engage in sensual, playful, and certainly not erotic touch. This approach sets you up for the traditional sex power struggle, with the man resenting lack of intercourse frequency and the woman feeling that her need for intimacy and touch is subverted by his intercourse focus. Like most power struggles, this is both unnecessary and unwise. Valuing each type of touch for itself, stemming from an awareness of choices for pleasurable connection, is a solid base for quality couple eroticism and intimacy (Exercise 9.3).

• • • • • • •

EXERCISE 9.3 VALUING PLEASURE AND TOUCH

Complete the following chart individually, then share your perspectives and preferences with your partner. First, what is the present percentage of affectionate/comfort, sensual, playful, erotic, and intercourse touch you actually experience. Be honest and forthcoming. The second part of the exercise is even more important. What is the amount and percentage of touch you really want for yourself and your relationship? This is a way to increase awareness of your needs, feelings, and preferences so you can understand and satisfy each other.

Touch Type	Current Percent of Touch	Percent of Touch You Want
Affectionate/Comforting Touch		
Sensual Touch		
Playful Touch		
Erotic Touch		
Intercourse Touch		

What has this exercise taught you about yourself, your partner, and the role and meaning of pleasurable touch in your sexual relationship? To finish this exercise, each partner can make one request to add pleasurable touch to your sexual repertoire. Remember the difference between a request and a demand. A demand says you have to do it my way or there will be a price to pay (negative consequence). A request is based on a positive influence process; your partner can respond affirmatively, make a modification, or say no and not be afraid of resentment or retribution.

In making a request, what can you agree to try in order to build a variable, flexible approach to pleasure-oriented touching? Ideally, you develop comfort with all dimensions of touching, continuing to blend and utilize at least three or four dimensions of touch. When you have only affection and intercourse, your couple sexual repertoire is vulnerable to limited pleasure and to being subverted by the traditional "intercourse or nothing" power struggle.

We suggest the partner who initiates a sensual, playful, or erotic date chooses whether to stay with this dimension or allow it to serve as a bridge to intercourse. Ideally, both of you would feel comfortable initiating touch and feel free to stay with a pleasurable dimension or transition to intercourse.

Sexually satisfied couples enjoy touch for affection and sensual pleasure (Kleinplatz, 1996). You learn that an initial focus on relaxation and touch is the foundation for sensual response, and that sensual pleasure is the foundation for sexual arousal and heightened eroticism. Pleasure is the core value for GES. Although sex function, including intercourse and orgasm, is very important, it is best understood through the focus of desire, pleasure, eroticism, and satisfaction

KAREN AND JUAN

Cross-cultural couples experience a number of challenges, including sexuality. Karen grew up in a lower socioeconomic class family in Oklahoma. She was highly motivated to be the first in her family to graduate college and enjoy the benefits of middle-class life. After college, she left her home state to create a career and life on the East Coast. She met Juan, who was in the United States on a work visa. Sharing your lives and dreams in a new relationship is very energizing. They were a stereotypic romantic love/ passionate sex/ idealized couple.

Their decision to marry was met by concern, but not opposition, in both families. Karen and Juan assured their respective families that they knew this would take communication, thoughtful exploration of issues, and perhaps counseling to ensure they would have a satisfying, stable marriage. They laid a solid foundation by discussing personal and cultural differences and reaching understandings and agreements in most areas.

Karen and Juan were surprised and perplexed that one of their strongest areas, sexuality, was now a major problem. Karen suggested they engage in focused, time-limited couple sex therapy.

Juan thought this unnecessary, but as sexual frequency diminished and sexual dissatisfaction rose, he was open to addressing sex issues with professional help. Karen and Juan consulted a psychologist who was also a certified marital and sex therapist. The first session involved both of them, followed by a psychological/relational/sexual history session with each alone. At the couple feedback session, the therapist pinpointed the major issue for Karen and Juan. The romantic love/passionate sex phase ended after 8 months, and they had not transitioned to a comfortable, functional couple sexual style.

Karen had hoped to have a complementary style in which each could initiate a sensual or sexual encounter, both valued intimacy and eroticism, and both were open to a range of pleasurable and sexual experiences. Juan had fallen into the traditional couple sexual style where he initiated intercourse and focused on frequency and intercourse performance. It was as if each was speaking a different sexual language, and they were caught in a power struggle of who was wrong.

In helping them construct a common sexual language based on pleasure, the therapist suggested that Juan initiate a sensual touch date and Karen a playful touch date without intercourse. This was particularly valuable for Juan, who experienced for the first time the joys of sensual pleasure separate from intercourse. Taking turns receiving sensual touch was a very positive experience. Karen and Juan accepted that his getting an erection as a natural response to pleasure was fine. His erection was not a demand for intercourse. Karen became aware that rather than welcoming Juan's erection as a symbol of his attraction and desire, she had lost interest/enjoyment and felt pressured for intercourse.

This insight was further developed during her playful date. Again, there was a prohibition on intercourse. This focus was on the playful dimension of four to six feelings of pleasure. Juan's erection and erotic flow was greater, and Karen felt panicky rather than pleased. This led to a crucial discussion about pleasure/function versus performance/intercourse. Juan was surprised by

Karen's negative reaction to his arousal/erection. It made him aware that what he'd viewed as her strange reaction was caused by perceived pressure and sexual demands.

The therapist asked whether Juan wanted to be Karen's intimate and erotic friend. Juan strongly affirmed that this was his intention. The question to Karen was how to change her understanding and interaction so that intimacy, pleasuring, and sexuality were a good part of their relationship. Karen rose to the challenge by saying she and Juan needed to speak the same sexual language, which meant needing to know what to do when Juan's desire or arousal was greater than hers. Was she a second-class sexual person who would always feel sexually pressured? The common ground was the focus on pleasure, and the common language was choice about sensual and sexual dimensions. Specifically, Juan's erection was a natural result of pleasurable touch (as was Karen's responsivity and lubrication). It was a positive symbol, not a performance demand. Touching could stay in the playful or sensual dimension, or it could flow into the erotic or intercourse dimension. Intercourse was a possibility but only as a comfortable choice for both of them. Pleasure can be and often is asynchronous, which is normal and healthy. Pressure or coercion is antithetical to the pleasuring process. This language and common ground made sense to Karen and Juan. Intimacy and sexuality constituted an area of their shared lives that could be a positive resource.

SUMMARY

The sexual "hype" in movies, talk shows, sex articles, and books seldom or never mentions the role of relaxation as the foundation for sexual comfort, pleasure, and function. We hope that after discussing these concepts, exercises, case illustrations, and suggestions, you realize the positive, integral role that relaxation can play in quality couple sexuality. Relaxation is the foundation of arousal, erotic flow, and orgasm. The prime function of physical and psychological relaxation is to set a comfortable, cooperative milieu to facilitate receptivity and responsivity to sensual and sexual pleasure.

The essence of quality couple sexuality is openness to giving and receiving five kinds of pleasurable touch. Based on relaxation, the GES pleasure principle emphasizes desire and satisfaction, including intercourse and orgasm. However, pleasure is overridden by an emphasis on perfect performance sex that calls for erection, intercourse, and orgasm at every encounter. This performance orientation can subvert desire and satisfaction and lead to sexual dysfunction. A challenge for healthy couples is to enjoy pleasure for itself as well as to use it as a bridge to intercourse and orgasm. Relaxation and non-demand pleasuring serve as the foundation for the variable, flexible couple sexuality that leads to enduring desire.

10

Flexibility and Variability Build Enduring Quality

Enduring sexual desire, quality, and optimal satisfaction require flexible attitudes, behaviors, and feelings. Adopting an attitude of flexibility will help you relish the exceptional sexual times, embrace the honest reality that things don't always go as we wish, that sex day-to-day varies in quality, and that your overall feelings as a couple are more important than any given sexual experience. Accept that your sexual feelings are variable, that they fluctuate from occasion to occasion, and that they are sometimes confusing. Regulate your feelings so they do not undermine flexibility or push you to negative behaviors. Sometimes you cooperate to celebrate joys in your bedroom, and at another time you cooperate to "make the best of it" when things don't go well.

Valuing variable, flexible couple sex is an essential feature of enduring quality and enhanced satisfaction—yet a challenge for most couples. The cultural view of sex is particularly one-dimensional. Both the traditional "hot sex" approach and the more contemporary "magic sex" notions focus on individual arousal with the promise that sex will be steamy and both partners will be orgasmic every time. These unreasonable expectations set up an inevitable disillusionment and sexual decline. The reality is that hot sex is wonderful but occasional, and the performance demand for it every time is destructive—especially for couples over 30.

SEXUAL FLEXIBILITY

With pleasure as the core, the majority of sexual experiences do flow to intercourse. However, when there is not an erotic flow to intercourse, you can transition (without panicking or apologizing) to an erotic, non-intercourse scenario or a sensual, cuddly scenario. Healthy couples adapt, accept that the quality of sex is variable, and develop flexibility that satisfies both partners and ensures desire, pleasure, and satisfaction into your 60s, 70s, and 80s (Foley, 2004).

Sexual flexibility is a major feature of sexual quality and satisfaction, and supports being a strong, resilient, intimate team. Couple flexibility can be blocked by narrow purposes for sex, rigid styles of sexual arousal, and the fear of sexual dysfunction in long-term relationships caused by over-familiarity, better known as boredom. Learning sexual flexibility involves:

- Appreciating the inherent variability of couple sex,
- Valuing at least four of five main reasons for having sex,
- Blending three arousal styles, and
- Learning psychosexual skills to build flexibility and manage sex frustrations and difficulties.

HEALTHY, SATISFYING SEX VARIES IN QUALITY

The sexual ideal portrayed in R-rated movies shows both people highly turned-on before any touching begins, having easy and dramatic arousal, and multiple orgasms. Perfect performance! If you are lucky enough to have Hollywood-quality couple sex once a month, you are more fortunate than 95% of couples.

A highly valued experience is for both partners to feel desire, become aroused, and experience orgasm. Among happily married, sexually satisfied couples, this occurs in 35 to 45% of encounters. In another 20 to 25% of encounters, the sex is better for one partner than the other, but it's a good couple experience. For another 10 to 15% of encounters, the sex is okay but nothing special. It is crucially important to be aware that in 5 to 15% of encounters, the sex is dissatisfying or dysfunctional—a statistic reported by very satisfied couples (Laumann et al., 1994; see Table 10.1). You need not panic when it occurs. Realizing that this is normal, healthy variability can free you from unrealistic sex demands. This is especially important for the man when intercourse/orgasm doesn't happen for whatever reason. He is challenged to regulate his physiological frustration in a pro-intimate way. A common couple strategy is warmly embracing and scheduling a rain check—a commitment to get together when you are receptive and responsive. It can help to think it's a "postponement," not a failure or "rejection." Again, the theme is not just to accept sexual variability and flexibility, but to embrace it as normal and healthy. These realistic expectations, empathy, and cooperation to "make the best of it" promote acceptance and satisfaction. The crucial skill is to not let frustration alienate you, lead to arguing, or leaving the bed. You're an intimate team.

Accepting, even valuing, variable sexual experiences and abandoning the need for perfect performance guards against sexual dysfunction by overcoming performance pressure, fear of failure, and rejection. Positive, realistic sexual expectations engender sexual acceptance and immunize you from sexual problems, especially with aging.

Table 10.1 The Quality of Sex in Well-Functioning, Satisfied Married Couples

35–45%	Very satisfying
20–25%	Good (at least for one partner)
10–15%	Okay (unremarkable)
5–15%	Unsatisfying (or dysfunctional)

Sources: Frank, et al., 1978; Laumann et al., 1994

THE FIVE BASIC PURPOSES FOR SEX

An important tool to reinforce flexibility is appreciating the multiple reasons for having sex. There are five basic purposes for sex and they vary for partners in different situations at different times (Table 10.2). Awareness enhances understanding of the roles and meanings of healthy couple sex. Accept that you can be sexual for multiple and varying reasons, and cooperatively blend your sexual agenda. The five main purposes for sex are pleasure, emotional connection, stress reduction, self-esteem, and reproduction.

Reproduction is the "natural" biological function of sex. Stress and anxiety reduction is a common biopsychological purpose of sex for both women and men. Sensual enjoyment and pleasure constitute a basic function of sex in long-term, satisfying relationships. Individuals also seek enhancement of self-esteem through sex, and pursue feelings of self-worth, confidence, and pride in being a sexual person. Sex is also used for a variety of relationship dimensions such as love, affection, healing, and joy. In healthy relationships, these are positively motivated purposes. In distressed relationships, the purposes are often negative, including manipulation, control, proving something to self or partner, hurt, or revenge.

When the purpose for sex becomes singular or rigid (for example, sex only for romantic intimacy or for conception among couples in infertility treatment), sex can become distressing and dysfunctional. Another example is that one partner may engage in sex primarily for physical pleasure or stress reduction, while the other may be focused on self-esteem and love. The potential for conflict

Table 10.2 The Five Basic Purposes for Sex

---

1. *Pleasure*: Sex as a shared pleasure.

2. *Intimacy*: Sex as a means to reinforce and deepen closeness, connection.

3. *Stress relief*: Sex as a tension or anxiety reducer, especially to deal with the stresses of a shared life.

4. *Self-esteem*: Sex as a means to reinforce self-esteem and feelings of attraction (desirability).

5. *Reproduction*: Sex to achieve a planned, wanted pregnancy—the biological function of having a baby.

---

exists when you feel this difference in purpose and misinterpret it as selfishness. Acceptance of differences promotes cooperation and satisfaction.

You may pursue different purposes at different times. For example, at a particular time, a man may seek tension release prompted by testosterone and workday pressures, while the woman may seek the "emotional gains" (Basson, 2005) of self-esteem, satisfaction, and closeness. During the course of your sexual relationship, all five purposes are likely to come into play at different times. Often multiple purposes are pursued simultaneously.

BLENDING MULTIPLE PURPOSES

Much of the time the purpose of sex is to energize your bond on multiple levels and enhance feelings of desire and desirability. At other times, sex serves as a "safe harbor" while dealing with stresses such as illness, job loss, difficulty in parenting. Sex can be both a refuge and an energizer. You often attach multiple purposes to the same occasion. You may engage in sex with 40% of the purpose to feel physical pleasure, 40% for loving feelings, 20% for self-esteem, and 0% for procreation. Your partner may seek sex 50% for procreation, 20% for self-esteem, 10% for love, 10% for tension release, and 10% for pleasure. Realizing and accepting that you have sex for multiple and fluctuating purposes, avoiding unilateral and inflexible goals, clarifying your sexual agenda, and developing partner congruence enhance cooperation and sexual satisfaction.

The major sexual cue for both men and women is an involved, aroused partner.

Satisfied couples cooperate even when they are sexual for different reasons. Emotionally and sexually you are individuals, not clones of each other. It is important to recognize that it is normal for one or both partners to alter the purpose of the sexual experience during the encounter. For example, sex may begin as an intimate experience and shift to sharing pleasure and eroticism. Or sex for a stress-reducing orgasm for you shifts to a very bonding, intimate experience, while for your partner it's all about orgasm. Variable, flexible sex recognizes the primacy of pleasure but is open to variable roles and meanings.

THE THREE STYLES OF SEXUAL AROUSAL

Flexibility is invaluable when coping with periodic, normal sexual function difficulties such as low interest, lack of arousal (e.g., insufficient lubrication, erectile dysfunction), or difficulty being orgasmic. Appreciating different sexual arousal styles can help you be adaptable. There are three styles or methods of sexual arousal (Table 10.3). These styles are distinguished by the focus of your attention:

- Par*tner interaction* arousal focuses on partner interplay and visual stimulation.
- *Self-entrancement* arousal focuses on relaxing your body and enjoying the pleasurable sensations.
- *Role enactment* arousal focuses on role play, fantasy, surprise, playfulness, and unpredictability.

When you pursue arousal by *partner interaction,* you are active, talkative (romantic or sexy talk), energetic, have your eyes open, and are looking at your partner. This is the sexual style portrayed on television and in movies—spontaneous, passionate, and impulsive sex. You find pleasure and excitement by focusing attention

Table 10.3 The Three Arousal Styles

(1) **Partner Interaction Arousal**→ becoming aroused by focusing on your partner, his/her body, his/her responses, and the romantic-erotic interaction.

(2) **Self-Entrancement Arousal** → becoming aroused by focusing on your own body, the calming physical sensations, being receptive and responsive to touch, the sensual pleasure and erotic flow.

(3) **Role Enactment Arousal** → becoming aroused by your private imagination or fantasy, using external stimuli like sex toys or porn videos, role playing with your partner, surprises, playfulness, unpredictability, or acting out your fantasies.

on your partner's body and its responses, enjoying your interaction, and getting into the erotic flow. Each partner's arousal plays off the other's.

During arousal by sensual *self-entrancement,* you close your eyes, retreat within yourself, become quiet, and take in sensations. To your partner you may look detached and passive. You focus on your own body as the source of pleasure, accept touch, and slowly build arousal. Calm and relaxation, sensual routine, sameness, and stylized touch help you become aroused.

> **Different purposes for sexual encounters and different styles of arousal can complement one another and blend into flexible, satisfying sexual experiences.**

With *role enactment arousal* you concentrate on fantasy, variety (as simple as using a massage oil), experimentation, and/or sexual role-play such as dressing in sexy lingerie, pretending to be "tough" or "hard to get," acting out a scene from a movie or fantasy, "ravaging" your partner, having sex in new places, using "toys" such as a vibrator or dildo to build excitement through erotic playfulness. Role enactment brings variety and novelty to your everyday sex life.

AROUSAL STYLES AND GENDER

Partner interaction arousal exemplifies the classic male focus on visual eroticism, while self-entrancement is more common among women; each most likely is neurologically influenced (Fisher et al., 2002). However, men and women are capable of blending arousal styles for increased enjoyment and as a source of variety in a long-term relationship. Different purposes for a sexual encounter and different styles of arousal can complement each other and blend into flexible, satisfying sexual experiences. You are not clones of each other; nor do you need to be on the "same page" to have a satisfying sexual encounter. When you think there is only one purpose for sex or one way to get aroused, sex can become a burden when you're not in the mood. Appreciating the multiple purposes for sex and various styles of arousal ensures regular sex.

OVER-FAMILIARITY: THE FEAR OF BOREDOM

Both men and women in long-term relationships have fears of sexual over-familiarity. They worry that sexual feelings and behaviors will become predictable, monotonous, and routine, leading to dissatisfaction, and eventually sexual dysfunction. Having sex with your partner can become monotonous if you rely exclusively on partner interaction arousal. While familiarity has its benefits (aide to relaxation, sense of security), it does bring mellowing.

Boredom and a fear of sex dysfunction may be ineffectually addressed by focusing on excessive sexual novelty such as making demands (not requests) on your partner, increased use of pornography, sexual compulsivity, or sexual "acting out." These are self-defeating attempts to amplify partner interaction arousal (or on the other hand, sexually avoiding your partner to evade the concern). Worry about over-familiarity is ameliorated by learning and expanding your purposes for sex and your use of other styles of arousal, such as self-entrancement and role enactment, which can provide flexible sources of arousal, desire, and satisfaction.

PSYCHOSEXUAL SKILLS THAT PROMOTE QUALITY LOVEMAKING

Quality lovemaking requires skill. Valuable psychosexual skills, eight of which we detail below, include cognitions and behaviors that promote high-quality couple sexuality and become easier with practice.

Accept Change and Choose Adaptability

For enduring quality sexuality, you must adapt. Life continuously changes: your thoughts and feelings, friendships, work, family and children, health, community, social network, religious community.

Sexually satisfied couples intentionally embrace life changes.

These changes often bring anxiety. Your sexual relationship is no different. Adapting to changes in life and sex requires you to consciously appreciate and embrace change, in spite of your instinct to resist. Expecting there will be changes, and positively adapting to them, including sexuality, is one of the premier qualities of satisfaction. Sexually satisfied couples intentionally embrace and adjust to life changes. Accept the inherent variability of sexual quality and learn flexible cognitive, emotional, and behavioral lovemaking skills.

Appreciate the Role of Relaxation for Reliable Arousal

Physical and psychological relaxation—taking a break from the stresses of life—sets the mood for sex. Equally important is understanding the role of relaxation in sexual arousal. Relaxation promotes erections and facilitates ejaculatory control for men. If your erection wanes, relaxation and openness to touch allows you to regain arousal and erection. Relaxation allows a woman's body to transition from pleasure to arousal to erotic flow. Be mindful that anxiety and distraction interfere with erotic flow.

Remaining in a comfortable, relaxed, receptive physical state is particularly integral to the early stages of the self-entrancement pleasure/arousal process. Physical and mental relaxation facilitates receptivity and responsivity to sensual touch and high levels of erotic flow. Maintaining relaxed receptivity to manual, oral, or intercourse stimulation encourages sexual response. Relaxation itself does not result in orgasm; orgasm involves letting go and going with the erotic flow. However, relaxation is the foundation for your desire, sensuality, and sexual response.

Develop a Mutually Comfortable Level of Intimacy

The traditional belief was that the more intimacy, the better. Like many traditional sex beliefs, this is not just scientifically mistaken; it can be harmful. You need to balance relationship cohesion

> Too much intimacy can smother the spark of sexual desire. Balancing intimacy with autonomy is the key.

and individual autonomy, and appreciate that too much intimacy can smother the spark of sexual desire.

Do not de-eroticize your partner. The challenge is to balance intimacy with eroticism and find a mutually comfortable level of intimacy that facilitates sexual desire. A key psychosexual skill is reinforcing pro-sex feelings in both partners and seeing sex as something that energizes and bonds you. Avoid the traditional trap of sex as an intercourse-versus-intimacy power conflict. You want to balance both intimacy and eroticism.

Integrate Non-Demand Pleasuring Into Your Repertoire

Non-demand pleasuring involves valuing affectionate, sensual, and playful touch. Touch and sharing pleasure are more essential to quality couple sexuality than intercourse and orgasm. Each partner should develop his/her preferences in terms of affectionate/comforting touch (kissing, hugging, holding hands, reassuring embrace), sensual touch (non-genital cuddling and massage; feeling close and safe; touching before going to sleep or on awakening; rubbing back, foot, or head while listening to music or watching TV), and playful touch (mixing genital and non-genital touch, teasing and tempting gestures, bathing or showering together, romantic or erotic dancing). In other words, value pleasuring for itself, not just as "foreplay."

Few couples have the exact same preferences for non-demand pleasuring. This is not only normal but is, in fact, preferable. Differences can add spice and promote your variable, flexible couple sexual repertoire. Important sexual cooperation skills include establishing preference patterns of multiple versus single stimulation, mutual pleasuring versus taking turns, times and places to be sexual, and communicating choices of staying with a level of pleasure or using it as a bridge to sexual intercourse. The most crucial skill is attitudinal: the enjoyment of pleasure versus the pressure of performance.

Incorporate Flexible Lovemaking Skills

GES emphasizes being receptive and responsive to a variety of sensual and sexual activities rather than adhering to a rigid, totally predictable scenario. This concept of flexibility also extends to your approach to intercourse, which is a natural outcome of the pleasure/arousal/erotic flow process. Depending on preferences, either the man or woman can initiate and guide intromission. Often the transition to intercourse will be at high levels of erotic flow rather than moderate arousal. Most couples enjoy multiple stimulation during intercourse, but others prefer to focus on thrusting movements. Some couples at times enjoy "quiet intercourse," savoring the pleasant feelings of connection by pausing and resting with penis in vagina. While most stay with one position and follow one thrusting rhythm, others change positions and intercourse rhythm. This is not a matter of the "right" way or the "best" way, but personal and couple preferences.

Orgasm Orgasm is another example of variable, flexible couple sexuality. The traditional performance belief was the ideal scenario of mutual simultaneous orgasm during intercourse. In reality, the great majority of women find that their orgasmic response is variable. For example, less than 15% of women are orgasmic at each encounter. Among women who feel positive about their orgasmic pattern, the average is experiencing orgasm in 70% of sexual encounters. Only one in four women follow the male pattern of being singly orgasmic during intercourse without requiring additional stimulation. Perhaps the most "normalizing" information is that one in three women is never, or almost never, orgasmic during intercourse. This is a normal variation, not a sexual dysfunction. In fact, a large number of women find it easier to be orgasmic with manual and/or oral stimulation before intercourse, with their partner orgasmic during intercourse. Another variation is that 15 to 20% of women have a multi-orgasmic response pattern, usually with non-intercourse stimulation, but some with manual, oral, and intercourse stimulation. There is no one "right" way to be orgasmic. Honor your sexual uniqueness and enjoy variable, flexible orgasmic response. Usually, male orgasmic response is highly predictable, with a single orgasm during intercourse. However, with aging, male orgasmic response becomes more variable.

Erotic Flow   By its nature, especially with the growth of the partners and the maturing of the relationship, couple sex is inherently variable. This allows you to enjoy sexual flexibility in terms of desire, arousal, and orgasm, as well as explore the variable roles and meanings of sexuality. The prime focus is on sharing sexual pleasures rather than regarding sex as an individual performance. A helpful psychosexual skill guideline is the concept of erotic flow—desire leading to pleasure leading to arousal and eroticism. It is important to "go with the flow"; you can't force it. The analogy many couples find helpful is canoeing; you want to go with the flow of the water, not paddle against it.

Erotic Preferences   Flexibility is also promoted by appreciating your erotic preferences. Erotic scenarios and techniques can invigorate your sex life. Erotic videos, toys, or playing out fantasies are part of the role enactment arousal style. Again, this is a matter of personal and couple preference. It is important to feel comfortable and confident, whether you're using one arousal style or all three. Accept your own and your partner's preferences and integrate these in a way that promotes eroticism and satisfaction as an intimate team. Should you want to expand your sexual repertoire but feel some hesitancy, the healthy way is to be open to experimentation, to talk it over ahead of time to promote trust, and agree on a "safety net" (a way to stop if uncomfortable). You can veto a sexual activity and your partner will honor your veto. With a "safety net" you'll ensure more comfort and enjoyment together.

Manual, oral, rubbing, and vibrator stimulation are all valuable techniques to facilitate erotic flow—from 7 to 10 (orgasm) on the pleasure scale. Many couples are very enthusiastic about erotic stimulation to orgasm, while other couples emphasize orgasm during intercourse. Most women report it is easier to be orgasmic with erotic, non-intercourse sex. However, many women (and especially their partners) prefer to be orgasmic during intercourse.

You need to make a clear distinction between a preference and a demand. Some people prefer receiving oral sex to giving oral sex, although there are men who find giving cunnilingus more erotic than their partner feels when she receives oral sex. A specific psychosexual skill guideline is that unless arousal is at least a 6 and, preferably an 8, on the pleasure scale, oral sex can be self-conscious rather than experienced as pleasurable/erotic. Another factor not commonly understood is that a significant minority of men—perhaps 15 to 25%—are not turned-on by receiving oral sex.

Being orgasmic during erotic stimulation does not stop the woman from enjoying intercourse. In fact, many women enjoy intercourse more after having been orgasmic beforehand. However, if the man is orgasmic with manual or oral stimulation, intercourse is rarely possible at that encounter because there is a normal physiological refractory period where his erection wanes or "rests." Again, be aware of personal preferences; don't be controlled by myths or stereotypes. For example, some men find it highly erotic to have orgasm during oral sex and value the symbolism of the woman swallowing semen, while other men feel awkward and think they are wasting the pleasure of ejaculating intravaginally. Some women are fine with giving oral sex (fellatio) to orgasm but not with his ejaculating in their mouth. The core concept is accepting your partner's comfort level and preferences, and confronting intimate coercion. Remember, eroticism is meant to energize your sexuality, not be a power struggle where your sexual expression is achieved at the expense of your partner's sexual comfort.

Develop Alternative Sexual Scenarios

You can learn to value erotic, non-intercourse scenarios, as well as sensual and playful scenarios (Exercise 10.1). You can also learn to value both mutual and one-way scenarios rather than expect equality at each sexual encounter. While many people are only comfortable with intercourse and mutual outcomes, the majority of partners and couples appreciate a variety of scenarios and levels of satisfaction. For example:

- When the woman is not interested in intercourse, she is open to enjoying being the giving partner and manually pleasuring him to orgasm.
- She requests a prolonged pleasuring session so she can bask in sensual feelings and the encounter ends in his enjoying a slower form of intercourse.
- One partner finds the encounter erotically fulfilling while the other is content to "go along for the ride."
- She plays out a role enactment scenario that is very involving for her but neutral for him. Sexual involvement, response, and satisfaction can be quite variable and complex, both during specific encounters and over time.

• • • • • • •

EXERCISE 10.1 ALTERNATIVE SEXUAL SCENARIOS

In order to feel comfortable creating an erotic, non-intercourse or a sensual, cuddly scenario, you need to practice it several times. That's what this psychosexual skill exercise asks you to do.

> *We suggest that the woman initiate an erotic scenario and the man a sensual scenario. Ideally, you would play this out two or three times so that you are comfortable and confident with both scenarios. Some couples have a strong preference for one scenario over the other. For example, one couple finds mutual manual stimulation to orgasm highly erotic and satisfying. Another couple has a strong preference for a mutual cuddly, sensual scenario, which they agree provides almost as much bonding and energy as an intercourse experience. Still another couple's preference is for an alternative erotic scenario. She might orally stimulate him to orgasm, then choose whether she wants him to stimulate her to orgasm, hold her while she engages in self-stimulation, or perhaps just cuddle with him after he was orgasmic.*
>
> *In playing out erotic scenarios, the emphasis is on choice and sharing pleasure. What feels comfortable and fits you as sexual individuals and a sexual couple? Do not fall into the trap of coercion or feeling you have to perform for your partner. The whole idea behind variable, flexible GES is acceptance of couple sexuality as inherently variable while valuing intimacy, pleasure, and eroticism.*

A valuable family investment for couples with children (from babies to adolescents) is to go away at least once a year without children. The most important bond in a family is the husband-wife bond, which needs time and energy to flourish. Don't treat your sexual relationship with "benign neglect." Many couples find their best sexual times are when they are away without children, which offers the freedom and privacy for both nudity and a range of sensual, playful, erotic, and intercourse experiences.

Julian and Elizabeth   Couples fall into the trap of inhibited sexual desire. Contrary to popular mythology, this usually is not because of boredom with the same partner. It results from being mired in a predictable, routine sexual rut, as well as not placing clear value on couple sexuality. Ideally, as your relationship matures you feel more secure, so you can take emotional and sexual risks.

Julian and Elizabeth were a romantic love/passionate sex/idealized couple when they met at 24. Julian especially had grown tired of the dating scene and wanted a loving, secure relationship. Elizabeth had just left a 3-year relationship that started well and ended badly (a common pattern in young adult dating/sexual relationships). Elizabeth and Julian celebrated their emotional and sexual energy. After 8 months, they became engaged and hoped for a satisfying, stable marriage with healthy marital sex. They felt this special energy when they began cohabitating 4 months later, but less so when they married exactly 2 years and 10 days after their first date. Elizabeth felt this was caused by the stress of the wedding arrangements, especially the details of gifts and the pre- and post-wedding events. The marriage ceremony itself was a very special, energizing experience that provided special memories.

For most married couples, and those who cohabitate, the first 2 years together are challenging, and relationship satisfaction diminishes. This is a well-known scientific finding of which newly married couples are unaware. Elizabeth especially felt disillusioned by her decreased emotional satisfaction. Sexual frequency fell into a one to two times a week pattern. Sex was functional but not special or energizing. Routine sex that follows a standard script can be functional and orgasmic but does not fulfill two important roles of couple sexuality: to energize your bond and facilitate feelings of desire and desirability.

Rather than celebrate their second wedding anniversary with the traditional dinner and gifts, Elizabeth suggested they go on a 3-day camping trip. Julian was surprised and pleased since he was an avid camper. The first day they took a 3-hour hike through beautiful scenery. When they reached the mountaintop, they sat and talked about their hopes and dreams for the next year. Julian's main goal was to move from their condo to a townhouse, which Elizabeth affirmed. Her goals were complementary, not adversarial. She wanted each of them to commit time and energy to revitalizing emotional and sexual intimacy.

They had privacy on the mountaintop and this was a wonderful time and place to begin. Julian felt that this was the most energizing lovemaking they had since before the wedding. Certainly being sexual in the middle of the day on a mountaintop is special. Elizabeth said it was more than the time and place; she valued Julian's "being there now" and putting energy into their intimate relationship. Being aware, awake, and feeling alive is so much better than routine late-night sex.

Elizabeth and Julian realized that they were spending less time talking about themselves, their feelings, hopes, and desires, doing less sensual and playful touching, and engaging in less energetic lovemaking. At its core, sexuality is about sharing pleasure. Even as a young married couple, Julian and Elizabeth could enjoy variable, flexible couple sexuality rather than be stuck in a predictable foreplay and intercourse routine. Julian agreed and was surprised and pleased that she brought this up in a positive manner rather than complaining and blaming.

Julian's male friends continually joked about and denigrated marriage and marital sex. He, too, had been frustrated by the decreased connection and sexual vitality. Julian was open to working as an intimate team to revitalize desire, pleasure, and satisfaction.

The next 2 days included hiking, talking, playing, being sexual, and especially making future plans. They agreed that the next year would be an ideal time to conceive a planned, wanted baby. Elizabeth and Julian had a joint commitment to beat the odds and maintain a vital, satisfying marital and sexual bond throughout parenting. They realized it would be so much easier to reach that goal if they adopted a variable, flexible approach to intimacy, pleasuring, and eroticism.

Ensure Flexible Intercourse Stimulation

Guidelines for intercourse can help enhance your satisfaction (Exercise 10.2).

Identify Mutual Preferences   What are your individual and couple preferences for intercourse positions? Some couples prefer man on top, while other couples have two or three preferred positions (woman on top, side-rear entry, and sitting-kneeling) and on occasion will experiment with additional variations. Other couples treat intercourse like Baskin-Robbins' 31 ice cream flavors: they like to try all varieties (and switch two or three times during an encounter), plus make up ones of their own. What is comfortable and functional for you? The traditional couple sexual style favors man-on-top intercourse, while the emotionally expressive couple sexual style finds excitement in trying variations. Remember, intercourse is about mutual sharing of pleasure and eroticism, not to prove something to yourself or your partner.

Multiple Stimulation   Another intercourse guideline involves a preference for multiple stimulation during intercourse rather than a focus solely on thrusting (whether slow, rhythmic thrusting or hard, fast thrusting). Many men and younger couples prefer focused thrusting, but the majority of couples prefer multiple stimulation during intercourse. Women who experience orgasm during intercourse usually find that multiple stimulation is key (especially use of his fingers, her fingers, or a vibrator) for additional clitoral stimulation. Many women find that providing erotic stimulation for him (testicle stimulation, kissing, and back scratching) enhances their arousal. Other women find that instead of or in addition to giving stimulation, receiving multiple stimulation (breast or anal stimulation, French kissing) enhances erotic flow.

Erotic Fantasy   The most used, and the most controversial, technique for multiple stimulation is use of erotic fantasies. By their nature, erotic fantasies are not "politically correct." You do not fantasize about intercourse with your partner in the bedroom using the missionary position. As many as 70% of men and 50% of women regularly or occasionally use erotic fantasies during partner sex. There are two important guidelines about healthy use of erotic fantasies. First, fantasy and behavior are separate realms. For most people most of the time, the charge of the erotic fantasy is decreased or even eliminated when they try to act it out. Typically, it is a better fantasy than real-life behavior. Second, there is no reason to feel guilty or ashamed about your erotic fantasies. Some people avoid distraction or "play it safe" by limiting fantasies to unattainable people or scenarios; that is, persons or situations (e.g., movie star, space station) that are not a part of your real life so it does not become an actual enticement. Erotic fantasies serve as a bridge to sexual desire and enhance erotic flow to orgasm, making you more receptive and responsive.

• • • • • • •

EXERCISE 10.2 ENRICHING YOUR LOVEMAKING STYLE AND PSYCHOSEXUAL SKILLS

This exercise asks you to be personal and concrete about what lovemaking (psychosexual) skills would enhance your life and sexual relationship. This is a personal list-making, discussion, and implementation exercise.

First, each of you should list at least one and up to three psychosexual skill strategies or techniques that you want to add to your couple sexual style. Be specific about what you want to try in the present; don't complain about the past or blame your partner. Developing sexually healthy attitudes, behaviors, and feelings is a one-two combination. You need to take responsibility for your own sexual behavior, then work as an intimate team to develop comfort and confidence with the new psychosexual skill.

The second phase of this exercise is a couple discussion about your partner's request(s). You can accept it, modify it, or say you can't do this, that it violates your sense of self as a sexual person, or you don't think it would be good for you as a sexual couple. Ultimately, sex is an interpersonal process and requires cooperation as an intimate team. Find at least one and up to three psychosexual skills you agree on adopting.

The third phase is the most important: implementation. Reading, thinking, talking about sexuality is crucially important, but implementing meaningful sexual change is at the core of quality couple sexuality. This requires being open about sexual desire, pleasure, and satisfaction; practicing to build comfort and confidence; and working as an intimate team to build a strong pattern of resilient desire, arousal, erotic flow, intercourse, and orgasm. Perfect sexual performance is the enemy of genuine sexual change. The key is to adopt the new psychosexual skill into your variable, flexible GES couple sexual style.

Enjoy Afterplay and Satisfaction

Afterplay is greatly underappreciated, even an ignored dimension of quality couple sexuality although it is a crucial factor in sexual satisfaction. Most often, afterplay consists of a brief hug, "I love you," and off to sleep. Sometimes that's fine, but a more meaningful interaction is often of value.

> **Afterplay is a crucial factor in sexual satisfaction.**

Traditionally, women have focused on emotional satisfaction more than men, and complained more about afterplay being ignored. In truth, afterplay has value for both partners, separately and as a couple. You've just shared an intense physical experience, and you can share the "coming down" experience. Some couples enjoy using this time to voice their hopes and dreams. Others view this time as an opportunity to discuss a couple weekend away or plan a family vacation. Many simply hold and gently caress each other, savoring the connection.

It can be special to have your own distinctive collection of afterplay scenarios. What are some possible examples? They can be as elaborate as taking a run after a sexual encounter, showering together, or sitting on the deck discussing couple issues in a cooperative, problem-solving manner. It can be spending 5 or 10 minutes lying and cuddling and sharing positive feelings, or popping microwave popcorn and sitting in bed together munching and talking. Some couples develop idiosyncratic scenarios such as putting on their favorite music, having a spitball fight, looking at family photos, watching a favorite scene from a romantic movie, or reading poetry to their partner. Most couples focus afterplay scenarios on touch and quiet talk. This can include lying together and holding hands, sharing loving feelings or intimate memories, moving to the "spoon" position and breathing together, or putting your head on his/her chest and listening to your partner's heart beat.

Another potential role of afterplay is sexually driven. If the woman (or sometimes with aging, the man) was not orgasmic during the pleasuring or intercourse phase and is desirous of orgasm, this can occur during afterplay. She can ask her partner to continue erotic stimulation, ask him to hold her while she engages in self-stimulation, or use vibrator stimulation while he kisses or strokes her.

Afterplay can involve a number of roles and meanings, depending on the couple and situation. For most couples, afterplay enhances your sexual experience, solidifies your connection, and increases sexual satisfaction. As with other components of lovemaking, rather than rigid rules that apply to all couples, we suggest a range of experiences to add variability, flexibility, and satisfaction to your sexual relationship. Afterplay is quality couple time.

Rachel and Brad: Inspired and Flexible Coping with Infertility   When Rachel and Brad met 2 years after college, they were an optimistic, fun-loving couple who were focused on their careers and making a life in their chosen city, Portland, Maine. Rachel had grown up in Boston and Brad across the country in New Mexico. Each had chosen Portland after college because they wanted a mid-size city within easy reach of beautiful four-season outdoor activities. Now, 8 years later, with 6 years of marriage behind them, they were dealing with the hardest sexual issue couples have to confront—infertility.

Rachel found this paradoxical and unfair. Since adolescence she had received a barrage of information on how to avoid an unwanted pregnancy. She and Brad wanted a planned child, which both assumed would be easy and natural. Instead, they were struggling with infertility treatments. The gynecologist and the infertility team of nurses and technicians were professional and supportive. They praised Rachel and Brad for being motivated, good patients who were addressing this problem in their early 30s rather than procrastinating.

No other sexual issue (including affairs and dysfunction) is more difficult for most relationships than infertility. Brad and Rachel were committed to maintaining their intimacy while dealing with this issue. They were active patients and were aware that more than 80% of couples who are in infertility treatment for 2 or more years develop both relational and sexual problems. Brad and Rachel tried to deal with infertility as an intimate team that was jointly facing a health problem. They stayed away from the trap of "whose fault is it," assigning blame, or feeling guilty. They remained focused on using all their health resources to solve the fertility problem.

In college Brad had taken a human sexuality class, Rachel had taken a love and communication class through her young adult church group, and as a couple they had taken a skill-based, problem-solving premarital program online. Early in their marriage, they developed a complementary couple sexual style. At the onset of the infertility treatment, they agreed that sex during the high probability week was best approached in a functional manner, not for fun. Sex on a biological timetable robs sexuality of pleasure.

It was Rachel who introduced the strategy that served them well throughout the infertility treatment. After the high probability week, they would devote the next week to sharing pleasure and eroticism to reenergize their intimate relationship. When they found they were not pregnant, they would devote two to three days to sharing sad feelings and comforting touch. The week before the next high probability week was their fun, sexually playful week to steel them for the high probability week.

After almost three years, Rachel and Brad became pregnant using the IVF (in vitro fertilization) process. Rachel told Brad she needed him to be involved and sexual throughout the pregnancy. Sex is most challenging during the third trimester since it is uncomfortable or impossible to have intercourse using the man-on-top or woman-on-top position. Rachel enjoyed intercourse using the sitting-kneeling position because there was no pressure on her stomach and both she and Brad had hands free to engage in multiple stimulation. They utilized mutual and one-way erotic sex, sensual touching, and side-rear entry intercourse. Rachel and Brad were committed to beating the odds and maintaining a satisfying, stable marriage with vital, flexible couple sexuality throughout the parenting years.

WHAT TO DO WHEN SEX GOES POORLY

At some point in their lives, more than 90% of men, women, and couples report sexual concerns or dysfunction. At any given time, about 40% of women and 30% of men have specific sexual function problems (Table 10.4 and Table 10.5).

> At any given time, about 40% of women and 30% of men have specific sexual function problems.

Contrary to media hype, sexual problems, anxieties, and questions are an almost universal experience. It's a little known fact that among happily married, sexually functional couples, 5 to 15% of their sexual encounters are dissatisfying or dysfunctional. Couple problems include struggles over sexual frequency, conflicts about sexual scenarios or techniques, and sexual dissatisfaction.

So when you are experiencing sexual problems, rather than feeling inadequate or ashamed, accept that this is a common

Table 10.4 Women's Sexual Dysfunctions

Dysfunction	Frequency	Percent
Low desire	1 in 3	33.4
Inhibited orgasm	1 in 4	24.1
Sex not pleasurable	1 in 5	21.2
Pain with intercourse	1 in 7	14.4
Performance anxiety	1 in 10	11.5
Lubrication problems	1 in 10	10.4
Climax too soon	1 in 10	10.3

Source: National Health and Social Life Survey (1994).
N = 1,410; ages 19–59.

Table 10.5 Men's Sexual Dysfunctions

Dysfunction	Frequency	Percent
Premature ejaculation	1 in 4	28.5
Performance anxiety	1 in 6	17.0
Low desire	1 in 6	15.8
Erectile dysfunction	1 in 10	10.4
Ejaculatory inhibition	1 in 11	8.3
Sex not pleasurable	1 in 11	8.1
Pain during intercourse	1 in 33	3.0

Source: National Health and Social Life Survey (1994).
N = 1,410; ages 19–59.

occurrence and offers you an opportunity to cooperatively recognize, discuss, and develop variable, flexible scenarios. The harm occurs when couples withdraw or engage in blame-counterblame.

The most common chronic female sexual problems are inhibited sexual desire, non-orgasmic response, lack of subjective arousal, pain during intercourse, history of sexual trauma, and emotional or sexual alienation.

The most common chronic male sexual problems are premature ejaculation, inhibited sexual desire, erectile dysfunction, ejaculatory inhibition, compulsive masturbation (usually while viewing porn websites), and a sexual secret (variant arousal pattern, more confidence with masturbatory than couple sex, history of sexual trauma, and conflicts about sexual orientation).

COPING WITH SEXUAL DYSFUNCTION

So how does one approach female, male, and couple sexual problems? First, affirm that sex is an interpersonal (team) process in which the goal is to increase pleasure and satisfaction, not try to achieve perfect sex performance. In addressing sexual problems (whether his, hers, or ours), the strategy is a one-two combination of assuming responsibility for your own desire, arousal, and orgasm, and working together as an erotic team to encourage and share sexual pleasure and function. For example, the man who experiences premature ejaculation (PE) needs to carefully assess biological, psychological, and relational factors that interfere with enjoying intercourse and orgasm (Metz & McCarthy, 2003). Then he takes action to correct negative thinking and unrealistic expectations, increase general and pelvic muscle relaxation, learn to identify the point of ejaculatory inevitability, and engage in psychosexual skill exercises (e.g., "arousal continuum") to enhance ejaculatory control. If his PE developed after a period of good control, or he worries he has a medical problem, he should have a medical checkup with his physician to diagnose and treat possible medical causes (e.g., prostatitis). The woman takes an active role in the psychosexual skill exercises, especially using the stop-start technique, a different intercourse position, intercourse acclimation, and a different pattern of intercourse thrusting. Most important is to develop a couple sexual style that is comfortable and functional for both of you.

If the woman experiences pain during intercourse, it is her responsibility to assess biological factors (consult a gynecologist who specializes in vulva pain and assess psychological factors such as anticipatory anxiety, fear of intercourse, and pain sensitivity). She also attends to relational factors such as cooperation as an intimate team without fear of partner rejection. She can learn to view her partner as her sexual friend, use a vaginal lubricant, learn pelvic muscle relaxation ("Kegel" exercises), refrain from transitioning to intercourse until high arousal, and guide intromission.

Dissatisfying or dysfunctional sex becomes miserable sex when you are trapped in the vicious cycle of anticipatory anxiety, tense, performance-oriented intercourse, and blame-counterblame leading to sexual avoidance. Sexual problems can be resolved, or at least modified, if you adopt the stance of personal responsibility and function as an intimate, erotic team. It is important to adopt the variable, flexible GES approach rather than cling to the rigid pass-fail intercourse performance criterion.

To illustrate differences in sexual preferences, consider two examples of female erotic flow, Beth and Laurie. These differences are not a question of right or wrong, but two distinct preferences for relaxation, comfort, desire, pleasure, and arousal.

> One of the usually overlooked joys of sex is how variable and flexible it can be.

Beth had the more traditional pattern. She enjoyed beginning an encounter with a bath or back rub, where she could relax and settle into a comfortable milieu. She enjoyed the one-way format of self-entrancement arousal, with her partner providing multiple stimulation and she touching his hands and face and making purring sounds. Kissing was Beth's signal for integrating genital touch. She transitioned to receiving oral sex when her level of arousal was at least a 7 on the pleasure scale. Laurie had a very different initiation/desire/erotic pattern. She enjoyed when her partner started an encounter in a strong, assertive way. He focused on pleasuring her with seductive, erotic touch. He wanted to ensure that she was highly aroused before she slid his penis into her mouth as the transition to erotic flow.

One of the joys of sex is how variable and flexible it can be and how honoring your partner's feelings and preferences can be a turn-on for both of you. Sex truly is an intimate sharing. With aging, your body inevitably becomes less efficient, and the value of both relaxation and cooperation increases. Taking time to "settle in" and remaining open to non-demand pleasuring enhance sexual function. Lower physical efficiency is more than compensated for by increased non-demand pleasuring and intimate, erotic team-work. Quality couple sexuality comes from treating your body well throughout life, especially attending to physical relaxation and mindfulness amid life's stresses and tensions (Exercise 10.3).

• • • • • • •

EXERCISE 10.3 VALUING INTIMACY AND EROTICISM

This exercise facilitates being personal and concrete about the role and meaning of intimacy and eroticism to each of you, and how to integrate intimacy and eroticism into your relationship. It is "politically correct" to start with intimacy, but as a challenge to you let's start with eroticism.

Let the woman begin. Share with your partner the experience when you felt the most sexy, desirable, turned-on, and really let go sexually. What was it about you, him, the setting, the mood, external stimuli that allowed you to feel erotically charged? Share both the erotic scenario and techniques as well as what gave this experience special meaning and allowed you to let go and savor eroticism. What did you do to feel and invite eroticism? How did your partner invite, facilitate, and elicit your eroticism? In terms of your arousal preferences, is it partner interaction arousal, self-entrancement arousal, role enactment arousal, or a combination of arousal styles? In terms of the present and future, are there erotic scenarios and techniques that are special for you? How important are your partner's erotic feelings and response in creating your erotic receptivity and responsivity?

Then it is his turn to lead or design an erotic scenario. It is important to not make this a "tit for tat" experience or to prove how erotic you can be. Carefully consider the erotic scenarios and techniques you find most inviting and engaging. Is your preferred erotic scenario partner interaction arousal, self-entrancement arousal, or role enactment arousal? Once you've each enjoyed an erotic scenario, sit and talk. Make one to three requests of your partner to enhance eroticism in your relationship.

Now, let us focus on intimacy and this time the man initiates first. What allows you to feel safe, close, warm, and emotionally and physically open? Core to intimacy is acceptance as well as affectionate and sensual touch—a way of being with each other in a warm, meaningful manner. Intimacy is about safety and closeness, not sexual scenarios and techniques.

What do you as a man value about a physical and emotional intimate experience? What types of touch facilitate intimate feelings—holding hands, hugging, kissing, lying together in a trust position, giving or receiving a sensual massage, enjoying a Jacuzzi together, cuddling on the couch or in bed before going to sleep? What types of emotional feelings and expressions facilitate intimacy? Do it for yourself, not to impress or please your partner. For some men, verbalizing facilitates intimacy, for others the key is silence or breathing in tandem. For some men, the important emotion is feeling safe, for others it is predictability, and for still others it is feelings of acceptance.

Then, it is the woman's turn to share or design an intimacy experience. Again, this is not a "tit for tat" or who is right about intimacy. Physically, emotionally, and in terms of meaning, what allows you to feel intimate? Don't try to impress or lobby your partner, experience with him your unique way of feeling and experiencing intimacy.

Next have a couple discussion. What facilitates intimacy for you as a couple? Share your awareness and understanding of the different roles and meanings of intimacy.

The last phase of this exercise is the most challenging—how to integrate your new learnings into your couple sexual style. You want to experience both closeness and sexual energy. Rather than fall into the power struggles of intimacy versus eroticism or my preferences versus your preferences, establish a comfortable, functional couple sexuality that energizes both of you.

SUMMARY

Adaptability is essential to high-quality, satisfying sex. You owe it to yourself, your partner, and your sexual relationship to be free of the tyranny that the "perfect" intercourse performance model creates. When sex always must involve intercourse with a rock-hard erection and passionately wild partner response, the focus is on performance rather than pleasure and intimacy. By abandoning the "need" for perfect sex, following your own preferences as a couple, and adopting reasonable expectations, you free yourself and your couple sexuality as well as guard against sexual dysfunction by overcoming performance pressure, fear of failure, rejection, and sexual avoidance. To believe that sex, or any other human experience, should or could be perfect every time defies reality.

Flexibility and embracing variability builds enduring desire and sexual quality. Adopting the GES model ensures desire, pleasure, eroticism, and satisfaction. Highly satisfied couples adapt to the variety of changes life serves up, and embrace and value variable, flexible sexual experiences. You adapt by accepting multiple purposes and styles of arousal and intentionally integrating them with flexible psychosexual skills that result in deeper relationship intimacy and satisfaction.

11

Real-Life Sex
Regular, Playful, and Special

INTEGRATING SEX INTO REAL LIFE

In the GES model, sex is not an isolated fragment of your life. It is integrated into your daily life to create your unique couple intimacy. Sex is an indispensible, regular part of your relationship. Day-to-day living amidst life's responsibilities, joys, and stresses provides the opportunity to experience sexual interactions in a subtle yet distinctively personalized and enriched way.

GES encourages you to integrate your real lives into your sexual experiences. While on occasion sex can serve as an escape from the vicissitudes of life, it is essential that you do not detach or compartmentalize sex from your shared life. Simply living presents opportunities for sexual variety and uniqueness grounded on your life experiences.

Your stage in life and level of responsibility require situation-appropriate sexual expectations. While sex at times becomes routine, the quality of sex can be flavored and inspired by the circumstances inherent in your daily activities. These ordinarily small daily fluctuations offer subtle shades in variation and meaning to your sexual pleasures.

REALITY SEX IS BETTER THAN FANTASY SEX

A widespread notion is that sex ought to be superlative every time and at every age, especially during youth. This is a seductive fantasy, but not a reasonable sexual expectation. It sets you up for frustration and dissatisfaction. GES encourages you to have realistic sex throughout your life—sex that is fun, varying, invigorating, bonding, and satisfying. It is a curious truth that this "realistic sex" is an important element in helping you understand that your relationship is "normal" as well as special.

Life provides ever-changing opportunities to experience sex in a distinctively personalized and enriched way: sex on vacation or as part of a romantic evening or healing from disagreements; during pregnancy, periods of stress or illness, times of success and achievement, times of loneliness; after a class reunion, a good friend's wedding, conflict, business travel, a long absence because of military service, the funeral of a loved one; amid unemployment, disappointments,

> Life provides ever-changing opportunities to experience sex in subtle yet distinctively personalized and enriching ways.

adjustment to the "empty nest," changes that come with aging, increased togetherness after retirement. All these day-in, day-out scenarios with their joys and stresses have built-in opportunities to share intimacy and stimulate sexuality. When sex is situated well in your life, it can inspire you in myriad ways: through anticipation, sadness, excitement, healing, comfort, humor, encouragement, acceptance, and communion.

Some individuals view the notion of sharing sex during taxing or challenging times as insensitive, even disrespectful. For example, is it appropriate to use sex to reconnect during trauma or challenges such as after the death of a close friend in a car accident? Is the woman healthy who impulsively wants to have sex immediately after learning that her beloved father has suddenly died? Is she reaching out in a genuine and primal way? Can you embrace the complexity and depth of sexuality despite life's sometimes harsh reality and accept its sometimes primally powerful impulse for human comfort and solace?

What about when one partner is experiencing depressed feelings? For a period of weeks or months, you feel "down" and lack sexual desire. Touch can be of particular value at this time, whether for psychological support and closeness, as a means to increase responsivity, or to encourage orgasm as a tension reducer. Perhaps the most common pattern is that during these weeks or months, sex is more for your partner than for you; it serves as a means of maintaining intimate connection.

The integration of life events into lovemaking recognizes the multiple purposes for sex and the variety of meanings sex can encompass. In one instance, sex offers an anxiety release through orgasm, another time it offers tender affection and comfort during fatigue or trauma. On other occasions, sex allows escape and fun, emotional healing, or becomes a spiritual experience that allows a couple to gently and tenderly share sadness.

TIPS FOR INTEGRATING SEX AND REAL LIFE (TABLE 11.1)

Engage in Regular Sex

A requirement for blending real-life events and sex is regular frequency and a varied repertoire of intimacy, touching, and sexuality. Rather than being boring, lethargic, or perfunctory, sex on a regular basis in the context of your committed relationship is honest and genuine, adapted to the rhythm of your life. Sex can be lustful, respectful, passionate, tender, playful, soothing, and experimental. Couples who permit life's stresses and irritations to override regular sex are at risk of demoralization and alienation. Real-time sex produces enduring benefits like comfort, diversion, relaxation, trust, pleasure, cooperation, and emotional intimacy. For example, some elderly couples describe sex as "rebellion" against the limitations of physical aging (e.g., arthritis, fatigue).

Table 11.1 Tips for Integrating Sex and Real Life

1. Regular sex guarantees integration of life and sex.
(a) Don't allow the stresses of life to block regular sex.
(b) Regular sex provides an "intimacy blender" and enduring attachment.
(c) Reserve time for sex; don't be afraid to schedule "intimacy dates."
(d) Ensure that regular sex occurs at every stage of your life.
2. Attend to and ensure relationship quality.
3. Practice being a "Mutual Admiration Society."
4. Take prudent risks: Engage in emotional and sexual experimentation.
5. Confront performance demands and intimate coercion.
6. Promote playfulness and enjoy special sex.
7. Appreciate the depth of meaning for sex.
8. Be aware that you can have sexual satisfaction in your 60s, 70s, 80s, and beyond.

For many couples, deep respect for sex and their human experience includes transcendental, spiritual experiences that celebrate the meaning of life and death.

One of the reasons regular sex is essential to GES is that when the frequency of sex is a steady, "hell-or-high-water" reliable experience, it serves as an "intimacy blender" that integrates feelings and moods, pleasures and meanings amid the variety and challenges of your real life. Regular sex ensures a range and variety of feelings and meanings for sex that are at the heart of GES (Table 11.2).

Couples committed to GES do not keep moods or stresses from their bedroom. Rather, they come with you and can have a place in your lovemaking. When your partner is anxious (Angst Sex), a serene focus on physical relaxation and pleasure can bring tension release. When you are sad (Bad Mood Sex), the diversion to pleasure or the calmness of soothing touch brings tranquility. When irritated after an argument, the touch of reconciliation transforms the annoyance to contentment (Make-Up Sex). When anxiety, depression, or irritation is not allowed to prevent regular sex, GES plays an important role in acceptance and mood transformation. An awareness of the vulnerabilities and special moments in life (Transcendental Sex) allows you to experience specialness. There's "Spirited Sex" when you feel full of life and vigorous,

Table 11.2 Regular Sex Is Your Intimacy Blender

Sexual Environment	Example
"Spirited Sex"	when you feel full of life and vigorous.
"Standard Sex"	when life is uneventful, sex is a shared pleasure.
"Passionate Sex"	wild, lustful, animalistic, abandoned, shameless sex; taking your partner and being taken; rough, undisciplined, rowdy, raucous, unruly, noisy, boisterous sex.
"Make-up Sex"	after an argument.
"Compassionate Sex"	sex for soothing comfort after a major event such as the funeral of a loved one.
"Bad Mood Sex"	during despondent or glum moments.
"Angst Sex"	sex for tension or stress release.
"Vacation Sex"	on a holiday or escape trip.
"Role-Play Sex"	when you're "stretching" and experimental.
"Transcendent Sex"	sharing sex "under the stars," appreciation of the ultimate meaning of life, love, spirituality.

"Standard Sex" when life is uneventful, "Role-Play Sex" for variety and experimentation when bored, "Compassionate Sex" after the funeral of your close friend, "Vacation Sex" while on a holiday escape or weekend away, and "Passionate Sex" for those times you are each in the raw lust zone.

When your relationship is grounded in cooperation, regular sex can "seal the deal" of connection and ensure closeness. Studies suggest that certain "bonding" hormones (e.g., oxytocin) are released during sex. This provides a feedback loop: you love your partner, you have good-enough sex, you love your partner more. You accept that not every sexual encounter is intense but that each affirms your real life with real moods, and confirms your love as real people.

Reserve Time—and Energy—for Sex   Regular sex usually requires planning. Often, sex becomes a low priority, after everything else is taken care of: kids, school and careers, work requirements and stresses, social lives, community and religious responsibilities, relatives, yard work, shopping, hair cut, etc. Sex is easily displaced when we are exhausted, feeling "our work is never done." When we are living in this zone, sex is unlikely to be special or energizing. GES-motivated couples look for windows of opportunity in their busy, complicated lives. Sex sometime every Saturday, no matter the joys and stresses of the day—ill child, work stresses, flat tire, poor weather, house needs cleaning. Insist that sex will not be undermined by the responsibilities and vicissitudes of your life. It is "our time." Attentively save a little energy. You want to be alive, alert, and awake. Planning ahead helps you reserve energy and anticipate pleasure.

Don't be afraid to schedule sex. Spontaneous sex involves a common longing for a number of reasons, including the desire to be impulsive. Spontaneous sex feels "authentic" and "genuine." The passionate sense of "I'm wanted," "Take me," "I'm needed," or "I have to have you" is powerful. However, given the realities of most couples' hectic lives, it is not realistic to expect such moments will be frequent. Ensuring regular sex, including scheduling sex, intentionally accepts our moods, invites a mood adjustment, and brings a special value to your lovemaking. Each partner chooses to be there and wants to please the other, even when the mood is not "right." The desire for spontaneity is a desire for "Vacation Sex"—which, ironically, most couples have to schedule.

Attend to and Ensure Relationship Quality

Remember that your sexual feelings emanate from your relationship feelings, as well as your body. This is why we focus on the concepts that "the best sex is relational" and "being an intimate team is the environment for GES." Partners mindfully commit to relationship-building and growing and maintaining vitality. Deliberately reserve time for your relationship. Find moments to *talk specifically about your relationship itself* rather than work or family matters. Avoid criticism and belittling. Compliment each other frequently, and work together as life partners. Communicate sexual desires and feelings away from your bedroom, and express tenderness in ways that are not designed just to get sex. This is valuable not only for women, but also for men. Appreciate your partner and show it.

GES recognizes that couple sexuality is multifaceted both in terms of quality and meaning. The major role of healthy couple sexuality is to energize your bond and allow you to feel desire and desirable. Sexuality contributes 15 to 20% to relationship vitality and satisfaction. Sex cannot rescue your relationship, but it should not be allowed to subvert it. Powerful sexual experiences are not the norm, but do provide a special meaning and energy that reinforces valuing your partner and your intimate relationship.

Become a "Mutual Admiration Society"

A universal feature of satisfied couples is mutual admiration. Conversely, couples are incredulous to hear that there is no scientific evidence that complaining, criticism, or arguing is ever constructive. Some people mistakenly believe that arguing gets stuff out there and clears the air. There are constructive and positive ways to do this; criticism or complaining is not one of them. A continuing feature of satisfied couples is sharing appreciation and compliments—the mutual admiration society. "Thanks for picking up my clothes at the dry cleaners." "You handled our child well at dinner." "I hope work goes better for you today." "Thanks for helping me with that project." "You're an amazing lover." Being approving friends supports being intimate, erotic partners.

Take Emotional and Sexual Risks

Sexual encounters allow you to experience a special form of intimacy and vulnerability. Being emotionally open and revealing as well as physically naked with each other is a form of vulnerable sexuality. For example, Barry (McCarthy) treated a couple where the man was physically wounded and scarred during military combat. Physically and emotionally, his recovery was lengthy and challenging, involving several surgeries and extensive physical therapy. It was not until he took the risk of being naked with his wife so she could look at and touch his scars that they were able to talk about his post-traumatic stress disorder. Talking and touching was part of the healing process. It was difficult for both, yet an important element in their sexual life. The hard work to get to that point and to take the risk deepened their experience of acceptance, trust, and love. It was not "pretty" or easy but it was deeply meaningful and rebonding.

Risk-taking requires personal and relationship courage. The emotional risks start with you. A safe and comfortable milieu provides the context for taking risks. Can you accept your sexual feelings and preferences without embarrassment at one extreme or being demanding at the other extreme? Verbally and non-verbally, do you feel you deserve to make sexual requests of your partner? Do you trust that your partner has your best interest in mind and would not purposefully do something to sexually embarrass or put you down?

Emotional risks involve sharing who you are as a sexual woman or man. What types of touch are you receptive and responsive to? What scenarios and techniques provide an erotic charge for you? Is it okay to be sexually selfish? Are you con-

> **Sexual risks are more difficult but often very meaningful.**

fident enough in your self and with your partner to share socially unacceptable sexual feelings and fantasies whether about domination-submission, one-way erotic scenarios, lust, or sexual vulnerability?

Sexual risks are even more difficult but often very meaningful. Are you safe in your partner's hands? Can you try a self-entrancement or role-enactment scenario without feeling self-conscious? In R-rated and X-rated videos, no one is ever self-conscious, but most people do experience some degree of self-consciousness when taking sexual risks (unless they are highly aroused at the beginning). There is nothing more anti-erotic than self-consciousness. The key to successful sexual risk-taking is to accept your self-consciousness, and stay with the process for two or three times. By the third time you may enjoy the eroticism, with self-consciousness melting away.

Be aware that sexual risks or experimentation sometimes bomb. It made a better fantasy or looked better on the video than it felt as you played it out. The great advantage of your intimate relationship is that when you take a risk that doesn't work, you can feel embarrassed but you're confident in acceptance from your partner. The hope is that a good number of the risks to spice up your couple sexuality result in increased variety, playfulness, pleasure, and eroticism.

Confront Performance Demands and Intimate Coercion

Special and playful sex is all about enhancement and sharing. It involves special experiences, special energy, special sharing. Performance demands, especially intimate coercion, poison sex. Demanding sex one way or insisting on a specific erotic scenario is not about intimacy and sharing. It's about coercing your partner to prove something or an attempt to mask a covert fear of failure (e.g., erectile dysfunction, difficulty reaching orgasm). Rather than enhancing couple sexuality, this intimidates your partner's regard for himself or herself as a sexual person and destabilizes your sexual relationship. At the other extreme, the partner who rigidly avoids sex is practicing "covert coercion" or being "passive-aggressive." This needs to be confronted. When either polarizing position becomes a pattern, it fundamentally undermines you as an "intimate team." Couple therapy can be quite helpful in changing these destructive patterns. (Appendix A presents guidelines for choosing a therapist.)

Is it okay to use sex as a way to make up after an argument? Absolutely. Touch and sexuality are excellent ways to connect and reconnect. Touching can be warm and sensual, or it can be passionate and erotic. A healthy function of sexuality is to energize and motivate you to address and resolve emotional and practical conflicts.

One caveat regarding the positive recommendation about make-up sex is that some couples fall into a destructive pattern of interpersonal violence used as "foreplay." In other words, the make-up sex comes after physical aggression. This serves to reinforce the pattern of interpersonal conflict and physical fights. If this is the case, the healthy intervention is to set a hard-and-fast rule of no sexual contact of any type for at least 72 hours after an incident involving interpersonal violence.

When there is a clear agreement that coercion or pressure is totally unacceptable, it frees you as a couple to take emotional and sexual risks. The danger in a serious relationship is that you settle into a routine and so value safety that you de-eroticize your partner and relationship. Security provides the freedom to be playful and erotic. If intimate coercion persists, seeking couple therapy is a wise and important strategy (for resources, see Appendix A).

MARTHA AND COLE

Our culture emphasizes youth and special sex, especially in the first 2 years. You cheat yourself, your partner, and your relationship if you relegate playful and special sex to youth and new relationships.

Martha and Cole had been married for more than 45 years, had two adult children, and three grandchildren. They were a sexy, playful couple and had wonderful memories not only of their first 2 years, but also of the last 2 years.

They had a sexual play date at least twice a month, and Martha tried to do this every week. Martha still did part-time teaching to other nurses as well as lay public programs, working 15 to 20 hours a week. She valued her personal life, especially time with Cole. Cole had retired from his first career and was now very much enjoying doing commissioned writing projects in his second career. Ten years previously they built an enclosed porch on to their house, which provides privacy for their sexual play dates.

Nine times out of ten when Martha suggests a sexual date, Cole is receptive. Cole has embraced their sexual role reversal. At this time in their lives, Martha is the one more likely to initiate and is more easily aroused and orgasmic. Cole enjoys both the sexual playfulness and "piggy-backing" his arousal on hers. He especially likes it when Martha does something spontaneous or unexpected, like starting touching in bed and coaxing him into taking a sensuous shower with her or putting on his favorite oldies music. She phones him when he's writing, telling him in seductive detail how she wants him to undress her.

Another creative dimension Martha introduced is their special sexual language. When their children reached 3 or 4, Martha started to call intercourse, "playing around." These words were inviting and seductive but not inappropriate while parenting. Martha and Cole were affectionate in front of the children but never engaged in sensual or sexual touching around them.

One thing Cole especially value about their couple sexual style is their ability to "roll with the punches." He has fond memories of being sexual in their car while listening to the waves crash on the Pacific Ocean rocks during their first trip west and making love under the tree during their first Christmas in their new townhouse. Their first child had a medical emergency when she was 8 months old, which really scared them. Sex the next night was more about being grateful that she was okay than about sexual desire. A special memory was when the in-laws watched their toddler while Martha and Cole went on a 3-week trip to New Zealand. They proudly had sex in every place they stayed, which added a special spice to this trip. One of Cole's strongest sexual memories was celebrating his promotion at work with Martha's very special erotic scenario in which he was treated as a sexual "king."

In addition to special sexual events, Martha and Cole had an ongoing sexual life. Although flexible, Cole emphasized eroticism while Martha's forte was playfulness. Now, after more than 40 years, Martha was most often the initiator of both playful and erotic scenarios. Cole would listen to male friends complain about their partners, and felt he was a lucky man to enjoy such quality couple sexuality. Cole liked the fact that he and Martha had beaten the odds and looked forward to variable, flexible GES into their 80s. A healthy sex life was one of the things that made Cole and Martha feel good about their aging process.

One night as they were sitting on the deck with a glass of wine, Martha issued a sexual challenge to Cole. She wanted each of them to talk about their best sexual memories since their last child had left home. Cole likes games and challenges, and they agreed to meet on the deck two nights later and trade memories.

Cole chose a special bottle of wine, Martha made her signature crab appetizer, and they skipped the evening news to be with each other. Martha began with her favorite memory—being sexual the day after their daughter's wedding. It was a celebratory wedding and, after a family brunch, they took advantage of a late check-out and made love for more than an hour. Martha had always enjoyed being sexual in special places, and as the parents of the bride they had a splendiferous hotel room. The lovemaking wasn't just to celebrate the wedding, it was also a celebration of their marriage.

Cole's sexual memory was quite different. It was about the first Father's Day after his father had died. Although he enjoyed receiving presents from his children, Cole felt unsettled because he had not had the chance to talk things out with his father before his death. Cole felt a lot was left unsaid and unsettled. Sex that night was special and nurturing. Martha reassured Cole that he was a good man and a good father who could honor his father's legacy by being a role model for his children. As Cole shared the memory with Martha, he told her that the smartest thing he'd ever done in his life was marrying her. Instead of continuing the discussion, this intimate conversation served as a bridge to sexual desire and a very special sexual experience.

Play and Enjoy Special Sex

Partners who are happy together have moments of playfulness, lightheartedness, teasing, and humor (Smith, Snyder, Trull, & Monsma, 1988). Appreciate, however, that playfulness contributes more than a trivial component to your general and sexual health

(Metz & Lutz, 1990). Contented couples report that play serves several relationship purposes such as bonding with recreation (movies, tennis, a walk), intimacy promotion (special private meanings), and a tension release and conflict resolution strategy (self-teasing to soften an issue). These qualities can enrich the sexual mood and are part of your sexual climate. The special nature of couple sexual playfulness (such as affirming teasing or "nicknames" for sexual body parts) adds uniqueness to sexual experiences and personalizes your bedroom (Table 11.3).

Playfulness Twists Reality   Adult play can be defined as the cooperative attitude shared by you and your partner that imitates, exaggerates, or twists ordinary reality for your enjoyment (e.g., humor), to shape a situation to have unique meaning (e.g., double entendre or conflict resolution), or to celebrate special meanings as a couple (e.g., romance). Being playful is not a case of either you've got it or you don't. It is an attitude that you can nurture and expand. For example, increasing your sense of humor happens when you look for incongruity or irony in a situation—e.g., the proverbial pompous man slipping on the banana peel. Play allows you to perceive reality with an appreciation of irony, multiple meanings, ambiguity, exaggeration. Play cloaks nuances, exaggerates or embellishes, pretends in an "as if" manner. This can involve signals, symbols, and gestures with multiple levels of meanings, manifested by metaphor and simile. For example, you might respond with exaggeration, "Well, excu-u-u-se m-e-e-e...," in order to signal hurt and try to redirect the focus to cooperation

Table 11.3 The Value of Couple Playfulness

Couple playfulness promotes:
- mutual acceptance as intimate friends
- relaxation and trust, security, safety
- comfort with each other's body and lights-on nudity
- valuing sexual pleasure as much as function
- a deep valuing of your relationship; feeling exceptional, special
- the freedom to be yourself, to be creative without fear of judgment

when your partner sends a verbal barb. Or in the bedroom, one partner might pretend to be "hard to get" or a "tiger." Or if the woman feels exhausted but wants to please, she theatrically falls on the bed and says dramatically, "Yes, yes, yes, I must have you. But wait! Where did my energy go?" This sets the stage to collaborate about what works for you both this time.

Sexual Play Is a Skill You Individualize and Encourage   Like relationship play, sexual playfulness grows through several distinct stages that signal the deepening of intimacy. New relationships typically begin with *formal play*. This is socially scripted play such as dating and wild, movie-style sex. The next stage is *improvised play*, which takes formal play and adds your flavor such as a personal note in a greeting card, playing "footsie" at dinner, seductive teasing on a dance floor, romantic talk. With deepening intimacy you create your own private forms of idiosyncratic, *exclusive play*. Exclusive play personalizes sex with unique, private meanings, nicknames for body parts, tenderness that grows from your increasing communication and union. Exclusive play is a special feature of quality couple sexuality and feeling special.

You can intermix and vary forms of play. For example, you renew yourselves with creative, exclusive play; or at stagnant, routine times return to formal play—dates, dinner, dancing, concerts, sports. The three kinds of play provide resources for flexibility and freshness for you as a well-established couple.

Exclusive sexual playfulness is perhaps the most emotionally challenging—and most rewarding. It asks you to improvise in the bedroom, for example to share important emotional meanings and integrate them with playful touch. You could bring out your favorite snapshots, love poems, old family photos, wedding pictures, vacation photos, even sexy photos. As you share those materials, also share memories and feelings. Use touch to reinforce feelings, which makes this more authentic and meaningful.

Examples of Sexual Playfulness   Here are some examples couples report (see also Exercise 11.1):

- "At times we undress each other very slowly and playfully."
- "We dance erotically to our favorite rock music."
- "On vacation, I dress in my sexiest outfit, he in his suit, and we play strip poker."
- "We play in the Jacuzzi, mixing genital and non-genital touching."
- "When we're alone at home, sometimes we put on slow music and dance romantically."
- "We spend time tickling each other, which is sometimes sexual and sometimes not."
- "During dinner at our favorite restaurant, I'll pet his inner thigh."
- "I ask her for a private strip tease or lap dance."
- "We have nicknames for each other's body parts—'Grand Tetons' for her breasts; 'Big Ben' for my rod."
- "I kiss the back of her neck; she sometimes gently blows in my ear."
- "I run my fingers through his hair."
- "She strokes my middle finger during a movie."
- "I lightly kiss her eyes."
- "We touch each other 'sexually' while doing normal every-day things. We 'accidentally' touch each other."
- "I will expose myself at times in the house when we are alone."
- "She will give me a sneak peek when she teases."
- "We take showers together and will sometimes wash each other with sexual overtones."
- "I love to dress up for my husband in lacy clothes one time, then my regular underwear another."
- "We chase each other in the house. I will sneak up on her while she is changing."

- "I sometimes beg him in a playful way; I get down on my knees and beg dramatically for sex, that I have to have him. It's a spoof and a tease!"
- "When we are playful in the bedroom, I feel like we're really willing to please each other; that's why I think I so love this..."
- "I prize the way we can sometimes giggle and smile when we're making love. I feel so special then."

• • • • • • •

EXERCISE 11.1 SEXUAL NICKNAMES

The problem with formal sexual language is that it's long, Latin, and cold. There is nothing playful or inviting about words like "fellatio," "cunnilingus," or "intercourse." The slang terms "blow job," "go down on," "fucking" for some have a negative, almost put-down connotation. Why not make up your own language/nicknames such as "play with the family jewels," " come into my wonderful vaginal world," "climb the Grand Tetons," "admire Big Ben," "really know me," "share my wetness," "take me inside you," "let me be with you," "my beautiful parlor," "big whopper," "share my body."

See if you can find one or two favorite words/phrases for your erotic parts—penis, vagina, breasts, ass, testicles. What about favorite words/phrases for intercourse, oral sex, manual sex, erotic scenarios? Be sure your language is comfortable and inviting for both of you. Even better, combine the nicknames/ special language with playfulness, touching, and special experiences.

Playfulness Gives Special Meaning to Your Relationship   Playfulness characterizes your relationship with unique and special interactions. Appreciate that your playfulness is a unique, private communication system that only you share. You can feel comfortable, less self-conscious, more valued, and more open to share important feelings and emotions. Sexual playfulness promotes exclusive intimacy. Play enhances your cohesion, promotes trust, and helps your intimacy grow.

> **Appreciate that your playfulness is a special, private communication style that only you share.**

Playful Sexual Touch Comfort with and acceptance of playful sexuality opens a whole range of singular sexual experiences as well as helps maintain sexual flexibility and vitality. As you settle into a regular routine of sharing your lives and bodies, however, it is easy to drop your playful attitude and touch, and experience more sexual predictability and less intercourse. You fall into the trap of "If we're not going to go all the way, let's not get started" and settle for a relationship with limited "either-or"—affection or intercourse. A large number of couples, probably a majority, get stuck in the traditional male-female power struggle over frequency of intercourse. Both partners wistfully look back on the early days of their relationship when there was more playful touch and more intercourse.

The intercourse-or-nothing approach inhibits sexual openness and playfulness. Playful sexual touch is emotionally challenging because it requires that you convey your sexual feelings and desires, be open to your partner's feelings and desires, and be willing and able to engage in a variety of sexual scenarios and techniques. Sometimes playfulness is better for your partner than for you. That's okay. Giving and receiving gifts of pleasure is integral to quality couple sexuality. Playful touch is affectionate, sometimes sensual, sometimes genital, sometimes erotic, and sometimes intercourse. Yes, you can be playful before intercourse, during intercourse, and after intercourse. Keep in mind that intimate playfulness is always affirming and never sarcastic or hurtful. Your playful relationship and playful sex support cooperation, and keeps sexual desire alive and vital. Occasional playfulness is an important component of creating enduring desire. Set a goal for yourself to be able to value this aspect of your relationship and lovemaking: As one person expressed it, "I prize the way we can sometimes giggle and smile when we're making love. I feel so special then."

Appreciate the Spiritual Depth of Sexuality

Quality couple sexuality can play a number of roles in your life and bring special meaning to your relationship, including spiritual meaning. People talk of intermittent, optimal, transcendent qualities to sexual experiences that integrate intimacy, sexuality, and a sharing of each other's "soul" or essence (Kleinplatz et al., 2009). Spiritual sexuality can include everything from sharing comfort and sadness after the death of a sibling or friend, to using touching and sexuality as part of a healing process from a childhood emotional wound or a recent painful experience, to sharing a special moment such as becoming a parent or grandparent or rededicating your relationship. Some couples pray (place themselves in the presence of God) before or during sex, and others say they "feel the presence of God" in their joyful sexual moments. Sexual spirituality involves openness to a wide range of feelings and meanings—from fun, light heartedness and delight, to deep union with the universe, to transcendence and one's God.

> "To be playful and serious at the same time is possible; in fact, it defines the ideal mental condition."
> —John Dewey, American educator

Traditionally, sex was seen as a threat to people's religion and a very different domain than religiosity. In fact, many people believed (wrongly) that religion was anti-sexual. The last 30 years has seen a revolutionary change in religion, spirituality, and sexuality. Now, almost all religions are pro-sex in marriage. To the surprise of both scientists and religious groups, the data are clear that moderately religious couples report the highest sexual frequency and satisfaction. Those who advocate spirituality more than traditional religious observance are even more pro-sexual. Sexuality provides special spiritual, erotic, and relationship meanings.

You Can Be Sexual Even as You Age

Fears of aging can more accurately be described as fears of illness. As we age, illness becomes more common, along with sexual dysfunction. Men and women who report fair or poor health are much more likely to experience sex dysfunction (low desire, erectile dysfunction, non-orgasmic response, painful intercourse, ejaculatory inhibition, or premature ejaculation). As health status declines, sexual problems increase (Laumann et al., 1994). Maintaining a healthy body at every stage in life is very important. Just as important is to focus on what you can change—psychologically, relationally, and especially psychosexually. Fears of illness may be reasonable, but fears of aging are irrational. Unrealistic fears of sexual decline set up a self-fulfilling prophecy. If you expect decline, you probably will experience it. Accept your aging body and accept a human, variable, and flexible couple sexuality with aging.

Partner Sex Problems Can Subvert Your Sexuality

Your sexual health is also influenced by your partner's sexual health. When your partner has a health problem that influences his or her sexual health, it is essential that you be supportive so you can adapt as an intimate team. Flexible sexual scenarios need to be cooperative, whether this entails adapting to a brief illness such as the flu, or to significant changes such as menopause, cancer treatment, or arthritis. Your partner's problems are yours, and yours are your partner's. You are an intimate team. The healthy focus is on intimacy, pleasure, eroticism, satisfaction, and the GES approach.

SUMMARY

Real-life quality sex encourages you to value variable, flexible GES throughout your lives—whether you are young or old, healthy or dealing with an illness, dealing with passing stress or an ongoing life problem. While there is an occasional role for sex as an escape from the vicissitudes of life, most of the time couples do not compartmentalize sex from their daily lives and relationship. Life allows you to enjoy sex that is uniquely grounded on your life experiences. You can use sex as a celebration, an energizing force, a means of comfort, a fun respite from day-to-day life, a bonding experience, a stress reducer, a refuge, a means of reuniting after an argument or absence. Reliable sex frequency integrated into your daily lives becomes your relationship "intimacy blender." Quality couple sexuality uses life experiences to inspire your bedroom with joy, healing, acceptance, sadness, and encouragement. It can be your safe harbor among the distresses of life, as well as a meaningful way to celebrate the happiness of life.

The more we get away from the rigid concept that sex equals intercourse and is a pass-fail test, the better. The freedom to enjoy sexual play is a very important relational resource. Real life can have special sexual experiences; playful interactions; sensual or erotic scenarios; and moments appreciating the transcendent quality of intimate sex—all of which can enhance your desire, pleasure, eroticism, and satisfaction.

12

Good Enough Sex
Putting It All Together

Lifelong satisfying sex grows in a committed, supportive, intimate relationship. Your commitment to GES growth goals ensures that you are on this path at each stage in your life. This approach to sexual satisfaction counters the pervasive mechanical, flawless, perfect performance model of sex.

> **Never stop learning or growing as a sexual person or as a sexual couple.**

GES encourages different roles and meanings for your sexuality, including a focus on sexual pleasure, as well as sex function and accepting variable, flexible sexual feelings and experiences. We in no way want you to settle for boring or mediocre sex. We strongly support vital, optimally satisfying sex throughout your life.

Let your attitude be you will never stop learning or growing as a sexual person or as a sexual couple. Quality couple sexuality cannot be treated with benign neglect. Regularly put time and psychological energy into your intimate relationship so that it energizes your bond and reinforces desire and desirability. GES varies at different ages and different stages of your life. The GES approach allows you to appreciate optimal sexual experiences, as well as weather moments of doubt and disappointment.

EXPANDING AND DEEPENING YOUR RELATIONSHIP WITH GES

Throughout your life, being sexually comfortable and aware and balancing intimacy and eroticism establishes a solid base for your sexual relationship. As you grow older and your relationship matures, good physical health and healthy behavioral habits become more important, as does maintaining a positive body image, sexual self-esteem, relationship cooperation, and psychosexual skills. As your vascular and neurological systems become less efficient, psychological, relational, and psychosexual skill factors become more important for sexual function and satisfaction.

Embrace and enjoy sex at every age. When you are young, enjoy the vitality your bodies and lives bring to your relationship and that sex brings to your lives. As you grow older, one of the

Embrace and enjoy sex at every age.

distinct joys is that you need each other more in order to maintain vital, satisfying couple sexuality. This is a wonderful opportunity to deepen emotional intimacy, as well as a challenge for you, both individually and as a couple. Sexuality becomes a more genuine, more human encounter. The challenge is to use all your biological, psychological, relational, and psychosexual skill resources to blend sexuality into your life and relationship. Healthy thinking, especially age-appropriate sexual expectations, is a vital component of quality couple sexuality.

This ensures your accepting sexuality as a positive, invaluable part of your individual and couple long-term comfort, intimacy, pleasure, function, and confidence. As your relationship matures, empathy for each other and partner acceptance become more important in sexual satisfaction. You can embrace and enjoy sex at every age.

GES VULNERABILITIES AND CHALLENGES

Enduring desire, pleasure, eroticism, and satisfaction characterize quality couple sexuality at all ages. However, there are specific vulnerabilities and specific challenges that are age related.

GES at 25

The entertainment industry and media hype would have you believe that sex at 25 is simple, with no problems of any sort. After all, aren't the mid-20s the golden years for exciting sex?

Samantha and Geoff Samantha and Geoff are discovering that developing a couple sexual style as a cohabitating couple is a challenge. They met two summers ago at a beach house party and began dating that Fall. There is something exciting, almost magical, about being a couple in the throes of romantic love and passion. Although both had very demanding careers—Samantha as a second-year law student and Geoff as a financial analyst at a large company—they were able to make time for each other and enjoyed an active sex life. The following August, they agreed to share a room in a six-person group house. Living-together sex is more challenging than dating sex. Samantha and Geoff blamed their problems on logistics, as well as the emotional drama caused by roommates and their turbulent romantic relationships.

When Geoff and Samantha moved into their own apartment the next Fall, they naively hoped everything would return to "normal," especially their sex life. In truth, whether married or unmarried, dating or cohabitating, the challenge for couples in their 20s is to transition from the romantic love/passionate sex phase to being a serious couple who needs to create a unique couple sexual style. Although Geoff occasionally traveled for his new job at a mid-size company and Samantha had the stresses of a law firm associate, the major adjustment was sharing their lives 24/7. What was the role of touching and sex in this new life situation?

The great advantage of sex in your 20s is that your body can function with high efficacy and be very resilient. The great vulnerability is finding a balance between autonomy as a person and being a securely bonded couple. Specific to sex was the need to develop a pattern of touching, sex initiation, and frequency that was comfortable and functional for both.

Samantha prided herself on being a "pro-sexual woman." She was assertive both in her personal and professional life. She wanted to strike a positive balance, neither passive nor avoidant. For a period, Samantha regarded Geoff like she did the managing partner of the law firm. He always wanted more and no longer acknowledged her contributions. On his part, Geoff wistfully looked back on their early dating experiences and missed their intercourse frequency. He blamed the changes both on circumstances and Samantha.

In the late Fall, they attended the wedding of Geoff's oldest brother. Weddings are celebratory events and energizing for those attending. Geoff was close to his brother and very optimistic about this marriage. Samantha felt the newlyweds had created a genuine bond and seemed to be a comfortable and solid couple. This motivated Samantha to raise issues of intimacy, touching, and sexuality with Geoff. She felt they were less of an intimate team than they had been 18 months before. She wanted to revitalize feelings of sexual anticipation and desire. Geoff was glad she was positively motivated but didn't understand what the issue was other than infrequency. Geoff saw them as good people, a loving couple, pro-sexual, and felt he was an attentive, giving partner.

The problem was lack of freedom to touch and be playful, as well as a struggle over sexual frequency. Samantha felt Geoff did not understand her needs for touching and intimacy. Once he was aroused and erect, his need for intercourse and orgasm trumped her needs for intimacy and connection. Young couples without children have a typical intercourse frequency of two to three times a week, not daily intercourse or intercourse on demand (when he has an erection). Being a comfortable, touching, intimate team builds sexual anticipation and a sense of creativity, vitality, and unpredictability. This facilitates sexual desire. Good intentions and being a loving couple were genuine strengths for Geoff and Samantha. In addition, they needed freedom to choose to be sexual rather than engage in sex on demand. Geoff's erections were a natural and healthy response, but should not be a pressure for intercourse. The challenge for Samantha and Geoff was to increase communication and emotional intimacy, accommodate their emotional and physical energies, and thereby reinforce desire, pleasure, and satisfaction.

GES at 45

The greatest strength and biggest challenge for 45-year-old couples is to accept variable, flexible sexuality rather than depending on spontaneous erections and totally predictable intercourse.

Donna and Ray　Donna and Ray were a 45-year old-couple committed to meeting the challenge of adopting a variable, flexible approach to sexuality. This was Ray's second marriage and Donna's first. A lot of their energy was spent on parenting. Ray had a 23-year-old daughter from his first marriage, and the couple's children from this marriage were 16, 15, and 9. Donna and Ray realized that the husband-wife bond was the most important in the family and savored their couple time, especially time to be a sexual couple.

Like the great majority of men, Ray had his first experience of losing an erection in his 30s (38 to be exact). Both Ray and Donna were surprised by the erectile failure, and the sexual encounter ended in an awkward, unsatisfactory manner. It took 2 days, but Ray finally found the courage to tell Donna that he'd been tired and not desirous of sex. He had assumed that once sexually involved, he would become aroused and easily settle into an erotic flow. He reassured Donna that it was not her fault; nor was it a symbol of lack of attraction or love. Donna felt relieved. Rather than pretending it would never happen again, she asked what she could do and what they could do as a couple when erotic flow was weak and intercourse difficult. Like the majority of couples in their 40s, Donna and Ray were able to successfully transition from spontaneous, autonomous erections to enjoy pleasuring and erotic stimulation so that erections and intercourse were easy and more reliable.

The key is to enjoy sex even though intercourse is not 100% predictable. There were two strategies that allowed Donna and Ray to do this. First, they focused on sexuality as sharing pleasure and eroticism rather than intercourse as a pass-fail performance. Second, when there was no erotic flow to intercourse, Donna seamlessly made the transition to erotic manual stimulation to orgasm.

Healthy relationships, emotionally and sexually, are based on a positive influence process. As his erotic ally, Donna was able to influence Ray. She found it easier to be orgasmic during erotic, non-intercourse sex and, like the great majority of women, she was satisfied not having orgasm every time. Donna valued variable, flexible sex, and this made it easier for Ray to adopt GES in midlife.

The reality of two jobs, four children, a house, and a variety of activities and obligations is that unless you place appropriate importance on flexible, variable, sensual, playful, erotic, and intercourse experiences, it's easy to fall into the sexual avoidance trap. Donna and Ray were committed to enjoy broad-based sexuality. Of course, they most valued special sexual experiences, but they could accept and enjoy a range of sexual feelings and experiences.

GES at 65

The bad news is that by age 65, one in three couples has a non-sexual relationship. Contrary to media myths, this decision is almost always the man's, not the woman's or a joint decision. For some older men, sex performance is about frustration, embarrassment, and eventually avoidance. Their decision to give up on sex is made unilaterally and conveyed nonverbally. This is a loss for both partners individually and as a couple.

Vince and Anne   Vince and Anne were in the happy majority of 65-year-old couples who enjoyed variable, flexible GES. When sex did not flow to intercourse, Anne said she preferred a sensual scenario, Vince said he preferred taking a "rain check." In reality, the most common scenario was a non-intercourse erotic scenario, with both Vince and Anne being orgasmic.

Like most men over 60, Vince was taking medications and he understood that they could negatively affect his vascular system, causing sporadic ED. Yet, he still enjoyed subjective arousal, orgasm, and intermittent intercourse. Anne valued intercourse both physically and as an emotional symbol. Yet she was very affirmative of sensual and sexual alternatives. Anne's embrace of variable, flexible sexual expression was a tonic for Vince and dramatically reduced (although did not totally eliminate) performance anxiety. Vince was open to using all available resources, including pro-erection medications and erectile aids, to enhance arousal and intercourse. He used these in a back-up role rather than at each sexual opportunity. Vince's guideline was that if he had two sequential times without an erection sufficient for intercourse, he would use a pill or aide the next time to promote erectile function, to keep his mind focused on pleasure with Anne as well as take advantage of the placebo effect.

Anne supported Vince's active involvement in the sexual experience. She was open to his doing whatever he wanted as long as it drew him into the interaction rather than isolating him. Anne and Vince affirmed that sex brings them together and energizes their bond. Mutual satisfaction is the ultimate goal of quality couple sexuality.

GES at 85

The GES concepts of intimacy, realistic expectations and sex in real life, cooperation, being a team, focus on pleasure and savoring variable, flexible couple sexuality come to fruition for couples in their 80s. The bad news is that two of three couples have stopped being sexual by age 75. The very good news is that the couples who beat the odds and continue to enjoy sexuality in their 70s and 80s report high levels of satisfaction and truly value the vitality of being sexual, especially as a couple.

Susan and Norman   Susan and Norman were accepting of their aging process—Susan was 82 and Norman 85. Both enjoyed their emotional, physical, and sexual lives. Norman particularly felt like a healthy 85-year-old and was sorry for his friends in their 70s who'd given up on sex and felt old and used up. Continuing to value intimacy, touching, and sexuality facilitates a sense of physical and psychological well-being. Susan particularly enjoyed the gender role reversal that is common with aging couples; her arousal and orgasm was easier and more predictable than Norman's.

This was a second marriage for both, and they'd been married over 40 years. When they began as a sexual couple in their 40s, it was Norman who exhibited stronger desire and faster, more predictable arousal. Susan valued couple sex, but not as much as Norman. Now Norman, rather than feeling threatened by Susan's easier arousal and orgasm, wisely learned to "piggy-back" his arousal on Susan's. She enjoyed the fact that their sex was more intimate, interactive, and human. For satisfying sex, they needed each other. Norman especially likes that they've beaten the odds health-wise and have maintained desire, pleasure, eroticism, and satisfaction into their 80s and expects this will continue. If either one's health changed, they were confident they'd adapt. Susan especially likes the idea that touching and sexuality promotes feelings of being an intimate team and values this as a symbol of their vibrant aging.

HOW GES PROMOTES OPTIMUM SATISFACTION

GES principles are beneficial for you and your relationship throughout your lives. They can motivate you to value your real sex life, ensure a regular frequency for sexual experiences, and enhance your couple sexual style. Avoid a drift into unhealthy sexual attitudes, behaviors, or feelings. Rather than your sexual relationship being a concern or problem, it should be a source of pleasure, joy, rejuvenation, comfort, and contentment. GES realistically promises you exceptional quality and satisfaction but it does require positive, ongoing effort. You want sexuality to provide your relationship with vitality and satisfaction throughout your life.

When you integrate your growth goals—"put it all together"— GES promotes lifelong relationship and sexual satisfaction. Grounding sex as a positive, integral, and regular part of your life is validating and vitalizing. This realistic, positive thinking is not as easy as it might seem because you need to steel yourselves against the media hype, with its pressure to be someone you are not or pressure to sexually perform in ways that do not fit your actual body or honest sexual self. Are you free from superficial and unrealistic notions of sex? Take a moment to ask how well you are doing at this essential feature of GES.

GES sets the stage for sexual confidence and satisfaction. You are receptive to a range of meanings in your sex life, including sharing pleasure, deepening intimacy, reducing tension, reinforcing self-esteem and attractiveness, adding fun and playfulness, bringing comfort and consolation, and providing inspiring moments of transcendence.

Sexuality is so much more than intercourse and orgasm. As good as these pleasures are, there is a wealth of human experiences beyond. Complete Exercise 12.1 to help you appreciate GES benefits.

· · · · · · ·

EXERCISE 12.1 YOUR CHECKLIST
FOR MAINTAINING GES

Of all the exercises in this book, this is the most individualistic. Yet it ultimately needs to be done as a team.

We ask each of you to identify (write it out) what you need to do as a person to promote healthy biological, psychological, relational, and psychosexual skill factors at present and in the future to promote your quality couple sexuality. Be clear and concrete about specific sexual attitudes, behaviors, and feelings.

Next, with the same specificity and clarity, list biological, psychological, and relational factors that could subvert your individual and couple sexuality. Then discuss these positive and negative factors and make specific requests of your intimate ally to help you promote healthy sexuality and be your supporter in confronting unhealthy attitudes, behaviors, and feelings.

The reality of GES is that it requires of you—individually and as a couple—dedication, energy, and cooperation to maintain a vital and satisfying sexual relationship. Good intentions and communication are important, but not sufficient. You need to devote the time, channel psychological energy, and enact specific behaviors to nurture intimacy, pleasure, and satisfaction so that sexuality will enhance relationship vitality and security.

When you base your sexuality on accurate knowledge and positive thinking, mindfully remain open to a range of meanings, are committed to realistic sexual expectations and maintaining regular frequency, and value sexual pleasure, eroticism, and satisfaction, you ensure quality couple sexuality (Table 12.1).

Confidence and Self-Respect

You can feel proud and self-assured as a sexual person. Positive, realistic sexual expectations ameliorate embarrassment and shame about your body and sex.

You can feel proud and self-assured as a sexual person.

You confront notions that sex is "bad" and adopt thoughts and feelings that sex is "decent," including that wild, raw, and passionate sex with your lover is "good." You understand healthy sexuality as part of an unfeigned life. No longer bound by shame, no longer having to be someone different than who you really are, no longer

Table 12.1 Benefits of "Good-Enough Sex"

1. You feel self-assured and proud as a sexual person.
2. You understand and view your sex life as a normal part of life, not hype with pressure to be someone you are not.
3. You gain a sense of self-acceptance and view sex as a positive part of your honest, unfeigned life.
4. You accept your partner as an authentic person, not a mythic figure.
5. Your real life fits into your sex life and your sex, life into your real life.
6. With a pattern of regular sexual encounters, you ensure a full range of experiences, feelings, and meanings. Sex is your "intimacy blender."
7. You accept variable sex, and find and enjoy flexible ways of making love that fit your life situation.
8. You feel confidence in your sexual function, understanding that there are multiple reasons for sex and multiple ways of becoming aroused.
9. You have options and choices for pleasing yourself and each other.
10. You feel anxiety-free because your focus is on mutual pleasure as well as individual performance.
11. You feel comfortable with your partner because you cooperate as an intimate team and balance eroticism and intimacy.
12. Your comfort and security open you to explore and experience playfulness and novelty with acceptance and excitement. You expand your relationship and make "new meanings."
13. You are open to a variety of meanings in your sexual life—fun, pleasure, comfort, tension reduction, playfulness, consolation, transcendence.
14. You realize that Good-Enough Sex (GES) promotes realistic, optimal sexual quality for your relationship at every age.

anxiously fearing failure, and no longer pursuing perfection, you feel self assured, confident, and content.

Realism

You smile at the media and commercial hype about sex and enjoy your real life with real sex.

Self-Acceptance

Self-acceptance is based on your dignity and appreciation of being a healthy sexual partner. You value sex as a positive, integral, part of your life as an individual and couple. Your maturity about honest relationship sex instills a fundamental personal and couple acceptance.

Partner Acceptance

You accept your partner as an authentic emotional and sexual person, with strengths and vulnerabilities—not some mythic, ideal person who should be perfect. Together you incorporate sexuality into your relationship as intimate and erotic partners.

Real Life and Regular Sex Fit Together

A regular rhythm for couple sexual experiences ensures a full range of roles and meanings. The reliable frequency of sex reflects each partner's commitment to maintaining intimate connection in good and bad times. Regular sex in your real lives ensures your "intimacy blender." You can blend varying moods because you integrate sex into real life and real life into your sex. You don't allow the vicissitudes of life to keep you apart. At times you enjoy spirited sex, at others make-up, compassionate, angst, vacation, or transcendental sex. Sex can be "moody" in an exquisitely rich and intimate way, and it signals you don't have to be "perfect" because you accept and value each other as real individuals.

Variability

You can accept variable, flexible sex with its passionate and wild times, special and playful times, intimate and warm times, as well as mediocre and even dysfunctional times, without disillusionment or panic. You are open to finding variable, flexible ways of sharing pleasure that fits your feelings and life situation. You are committed to maintaining sexual desire, pleasure, and satisfaction as an integral part of your life and relationship. You want sexuality to contribute 15 to 20% to relationship vitality and satisfaction in your 20s, 40s, 60s, and 80s.

Flexibility

You feel confidence about sexual initiation and function because you understand that there are multiple purposes, roles, meanings, and arousal styles for sex, and multiple ways of sharing pleasure and eroticism. You can be flexible because you are an intimate team who are comfortable with options and choices for pleasing yourself and your partner.

Pleasure

You feel comfortable and receptive rather than pressured by anticipatory or performance anxiety. Your focus is on sexual pleasure rather than the demand for performance.

Teamwork to Balance Eroticism and Intimacy

You accept and trust your partner as your intimate and erotic friend. You can enjoy a range of sexual experiences, some of which are mutual, others better for one partner than the other, and others that are a gift to your partner. You have discovered your couple sexual style that balances intimacy and eroticism and where sexuality enhances your relationship.

Lifelong Optimal Sexuality

You realize that honest quality couple sexuality with enduring lifetime satisfaction is promoted and enhanced by embracing the values of the GES model.

SUMMARY

The GES biopsychosocial approach to sexual satisfaction integrates the reality of physiological and psychological dimensions (your thoughts, feelings and behavior), your relationship environment (identity, cooperation, and empathy), and psychosexual skills within your intimate relationship.

The cognitive-behavioral-emotional-relational model reminds us that sexual and relationship satisfaction is a based on how you think, which influences how you act and feel. GES guides you to emphasize realistic expectations for overcoming shame, positively valuing sex, promoting relationship cooperation, and ensuring genuine sexual satisfaction. GES promotes healthy thinking and highlights realistic, age-appropriate sexual expectations of your body, self, and relationship. Quality sexuality involves pleasure, confidence, and eroticism, which are the core sexual elements for sexual satisfaction. Sex fits into your real life, and your real life inspires your bedroom. Empathy and acceptance sustain long-term comfort, desire, and emotional and sexual satisfaction.

Relationship features of GES include appreciating the multiple facets and meanings of intimacy. Your relationship is the environment for quality couple sex, and empathy is the premier emotional "glue" for your sex life. Mutual pleasure and cooperation as an intimate team is an essential component of GES. This ensures enduring, high-quality couple sexuality. So be sexually "good enough"! You'll feel secure, self-accepting and loved—and your partner will, as well. Truly enjoy the sex you have and grow your intimacy with the GES guidelines. Review them periodically as a couple. Keep embracing your sexuality and expand its meaning for you and your relationship. Celebrate and enjoy your couple sexuality—for the rest of your life.

References

Adams, M. A., & Robinson, W. R. (2001). Shame reduction, affect regulation, and sexual boundary development: Essential building blocks of sexual addiction treatment. *Sexual Addiction and Compulsivity,* *8*, 45–78.

Barlow, D. H. (1988). *Anxiety and its disorders: The nature and treatment of anxiety and panic.* New York: Guilford Press.

Basson, R., (2001). Using a different model for female sexual response to address women's problematic low sexual desire. *Journal of Sex and Marital Therapy, 27*, 395–403.

Basson, R. (2007). Sexual desire/arousal disorders in women. In S. Leiblum (Ed.), *Principles and practice of sex therapy,* (4th ed., pp. 25–53). New York: Guilford.

Blum, D. (1998). *Sex on the brain: The biological differences between men and women.* New York: Penguin Books.

Boul, L., (2007). Sexual function and relationship satisfaction: An investigation into men's attitudes and perceptions. *Sexual and Relationship Therapy, 22*(2) May, 209–220.

Bradbury, T. N., & Fincham, F. D. (1993). Assessing dysfunctional cognition in marriage: A reconsideration of the Relationship Belief Inventory. *Psychological Assessment, 5*, 92–101.

Burns, L. H. (2006). Sexual counseling and infertility. In S. N. Covington & L. H. Burns, (2006), *Infertility counseling: A comprehensive handbook for clinicians* (pp. 212–235). New York: Cambridge University Press.

Buss, D. (1995). Psychological sex differences: Origins through sexual selection. *American Psychologist. 50*(3),164–168.

Byers, E. S., & Grenier, G. (2003). Premature or rapid ejaculation: Heterosexual couples' perceptions of male ejaculatory behavior. *Archives of Sex Behavior, 32*(3), 261–270.

Clinebell, H. J., & Clinebell C. H. (1979). *The intimate marriage.* New York: Harper & Row.

Cooper, A., & Marcus, I. D. (2003). Men who are not in control of their sexual behavior. In S. B. Levine, C. B. Risen, & S. E. Althof (Eds.), *Handbook of clinical sexuality for mental health professionals* (pp. 311–332). New York: Brunner-Routledge.

Dormont, Paul, personal communication.

Dewey, J. (2007). *How we think.* Mineola, NY: Dover.

Epstein, N., & Baucom, D. (2002). *Enhanced cognitive-behavioral therapy for couples.* Washington, DC: American Psychological Association.

Fichten, C. S., Spector, I., & Libman, E., (1988). Client attributions for sexual dysfunction. *Journal of Sex & Marital Therapy, 14*(3), 208–224.

Fisher, H. E., Aron, A., Mashek, D., Li, H., & Brown, L. L. (2002). Defining the brain systems of lust, romantic attraction, and attachment. *Archives of Sexual Behavior, 31*(5),413–419.

Fisher, H. (2004). *Why We Love: The nature and chemistry of romantic love.* New York: Holt Paperbacks.

Foley, S. (2004). *Sex and love for grown-ups.* New York: Sterling.

Frank, E., Anderson, A., & Rubinstein, D. (1978). Frequency of sexual dysfunction in "normal" couples. *New England Journal of Medicine, 229,* 111–115.

Gottman, J., Coan, J., Carrere, S., & Swanson, C. (1998). Predicting marital happiness and stability from newlywed interactions. *Journal of Marriage and the Family, 60,* 5–22.

Hamann, S., Herman, R. A., Nolan, C. L., & Wallen, K., (2004). Men and women differ in amygdale response to visual sexual stimuli. *Nature Neuroscience, 7*(4), 411–416.

Heiman, J. (2007). Orgasmic disorders in women. In S. Leiblum (Ed.). *Principles and practice of sex therapy* (4th ed., pp. 84–123). New York: Guilford.

Jacobson, N., & Christensen, A. (1998). *Acceptance and change in couple therapy.* New York: Norton.

Joannides, P. (2009). *The guide to getting it on* (6th edition). Waldport, OR: Goofy Foot Press.

Johnson, S. (2008). *Hold me tight.* Boston: Little-Brown.

Kaplan, H. (1974). *The new sex therapy.* New York: Brunner/Mazel.

Kirby, J. S., Baucom, D. H., & Peterman, M. A., (2007). An investigation of unmet intimacy needs in marital relationships. *Journal of Marital and Family Therapy. 31*(4), 313–325.

Kleinplatz, P. J. (1996). Transforming sex therapy: Integrating erotic potential. *Humanistic Psychologist, 24*(2), 190–202.

Kleinplatz, P. J., Ménard, A. D., Paquet, M.-P., Paradis, N., Campbell, M., Zuccarino, D., & Mehak, L. (2009). The components of optimal sexuality: A portrait of "great sex." *Canadian Journal of Human Sexuality, 18*(1–2), 1–13.

La Pera, G., & Nicastro, A. (1996). A new treatment for premature ejaculation: The rehabilitation of the pelvic floor. *Journal of Sex & Marital Therapy, 22*, 22–26.

Laumann, E. O., Gagnon, J. H., Michael, R. T., & Michaels, S. (1994). *The social organization of sexuality: Sexual practices in the United States.* Chicago: University of Chicago Press.

Leeds, R. (2001). The three most important criteria in diagnosing sexual addictions: Obsession, obsession, and obsession. *Sexual Addiction and Compulsivity, 8*, 215–226.

Lent, R. W. (2004). Toward a unifying theoretical and practical perspective on well-being and psychosocial adjustment. *Journal of Counseling Psychology, 51*(4), 482–509.

Lyubomirsky, S., Sheldon, K. M., & Schkade, D. (2005). Pursuing happiness: The architecture of sustainable change. *Review of General Psychology, 9*, 111–131.

Masters, W., & Johnson, V. (1970). *Human sexual inadequacy.* Boston: Little-Brown.

McCarthy, B., & Fucito, L. ((2005). Integrating medication, realistic expectations, and therapeutic interventions in the treatment of male sexual dysfunction. *Journal of Sex and Marital Therapy, 31*, 319–328.

McCarthy, B., & McCarthy, E. (2002). *Sexual awareness.* New York: Carroll and Graf.

McCarthy, B., & McCarthy, E. (*2003*). *Rekindling desire.* New York: Brunner/ Routledge.

McCarthy, B., & McCarthy, E. (2009). *Discovering your couple sexual style.* New York: Routledge.

McCarthy, B., & Metz, M.E. (2008). *Men's sexual health.* New York: Routledge.

McCarthy, B., & Metz, M.E. (2008). The cognitive-behavioral "Good-Enough Sex" model: A case illustration. *Sexual and Relationship Therapy, 23*(3), 227–234.

McCarthy, B., & McDonald, D. (2009). Assessment, treatment, and relapse prevention: Male hypoactive sexual desire disorder. *Journal of Sex and Marital Therapy, 35*, 56–67.

Metz, M. E. (1997). Playing for Intimacy, in *Working with Groups on Family Issues* (pp. 90–97), edited by S. S. Christian. Duluth, MN: Whole Person Associates.

Metz, M. E., & Epstein, N. (2002). The role of relationship conflict in sexual dysfunction. *Journal of Sex & Marital Therapy, 28*,139–164.

Metz, M. E., & Lutz, G. (1990). Dyadic playfulness differences between sexual and marital therapy couples. *Journal of Psychology and Human Sexuality, 3*(1), 167–182.

Metz, M. E., & McCarthy, B. (2004). *Coping with erectile dysfunction.* Oakland, CA: New Harbinger.

Metz, M. E., & McCarthy, B. (2008). "Eros & aging: Is Good-Enough Sex right for you?" *Family Networker*, July/August 2008, 55–61.

Metz, M. E., & McCarthy, B. (2007). The "Good-Enough Sex" model for men's and couple satisfaction. *Sexual and Relationship Therapy, 22*(3), 351–362.

Metz, M. E., & Seifert, Jr., M. H., (1993). Differences in men's and women's sexual health needs and expectations of physicians. *The Canadian Journal of Human Sexuality, 2*(2), 53–59.

O'Farrell, T. J., Choquette, K. A., Cutter, H. S. G., & Birchler, G. R. (1997). Sexual satisfaction and dysfunction in marriages of male alcoholics: Comparison with nonalcoholic maritally conflicted and nonconflicted couples. *Journal of Studies on Alcohol, 58,* 91–99.

Perel, E. (2006). *Mating in captivity.* New York: Harper-Collins.

Rolheiser, R. (1999). *The holy longing: The search for a Christian spirituality.* New York: Doubleday.

Sbrocco, T., Weisberg, R. B., Barlow, D. H., & Carter, M. M. (1997). The conceptual relationship between panic disorder and male erectile dysfunction. *Journal of Sex and Marital Therapy, 23,* 212–220.

Seligman, M. E., Rashid, T., & Parks, A., (2006). Positive psychology. *American Psychologist, 61*(8) 774–788.

Smith, G. T., Snyder, D. K., Trull, T. J., & Monsma, B. R. (1988). Predicting relationship satisfaction from couples' use of leisure time. *American Journal of Family Therapy, 16(1),* 3–13.

Spring, J. (2004). How *can I forgive you: The courage to forgive, the freedom not to.* New York: Harper-Collins.

Weiss, R., Hops, H., & Patterson, G. (1973). A framework for conceptualizing marital conflict, a technology for altering it, some data for evaluating it. In L. Hamerlynck, L. Handy, & E. Mash (Eds.), *Behavior change: Methodology, concepts and practice.* Champaign, IL: Research Press.

Winnicott, D. D. (1964). The *child, the family and the outside world.* Harmondsworth, England: Penguin.

Appendix A: Choosing an Individual, Couple, or Sex Therapist

This is a self-help book, but it is not a do-it-yourself therapy book. Individuals and couples are often reluctant to consult a therapist, feeling that to do so is a sign of craziness, a confession of inadequacy, or an admission that their life and relationship are in dire straits. In reality, seeking professional help is a sign of psychological wisdom and strength. Entering individual, couple, or sex therapy means that you realize there is a problem, and you have made a commitment to resolve the issues and promote individual and couple growth.

The mental health field can be confusing. Couple therapy and sex therapy are clinical subspecialties. They are offered by several groups of professionals, including marital therapists, psychologists, psychiatrists, social workers, and pastoral counselors. The professional background of the practitioner is less important than his or her competence in dealing with your sexual and other intimacy problems.

Many people have health insurance that provides coverage for mental health and thus can afford the services of a private practitioner. Those who do not have either the financial resources or insurance could consider a city or county mental health clinic, a university or medical school outpatient mental health clinic, or a family services center. Some clinics have a sliding fee scale (the fee is based on your ability to pay).

When choosing a therapist, be direct in asking about credentials and areas of expertise. Ask the clinician what the focus of the therapy will be, how long therapy can be expected to last, and whether the emphasis is specifically on sexual problems or more generally on individual, communication, or relationship issues. Be especially diligent in asking about credentials such as university degrees and licensing. Be wary of people who call themselves personal counselors, sex counselors, or personal coaches. There are poorly qualified persons—and some outright quacks—in any field.

One of the best ways to obtain a referral is to call or contact online a local professional organization such as a state psychological association, marriage and family therapy association, or mental health association. You can ask for a referral from a family physician, clergyman, imam, rabbi, or trusted friend. If you live near a university or medical school, call to find out what specialized psychological and sexual health services may be available.

For a *sex therapy* referral, contact the American Association of Sex Educators, Counselors, and Therapists (AASECT) at www.aasect.org or write or call for a list of certified sex therapists in your area: P.O. Box 5488, Richmond, VA 23220; Phone (804) 644-3288. Another resource is the Society for Sex Therapy and Research (SSTAR) at www.sstarnet.org

For a *marital therapist*, check the Internet site for the American Association for Marriage and Family Therapy (AAMFT) at www.therapistlocator.net or the Association for Behavioral and Cognitive Therapies (ABCT) at www.abct.org. Another good resource is the National Registry of Marriage Friendly Therapists, who are dedicated to helping relationships succeed if possible: www.marriagefriendlytherapists.com. If you are looking for a psychologist who can provide individual therapy for anxiety, depression, behavioral health, or other psychological issues, we suggest the National Registry of Health Service Providers in Psychology: www.findapsychologist.org.

Feel free to talk with two or three therapists before deciding with whom to work. Be aware of your level of comfort with the therapist, degree of rapport, whether the therapist has special skill working with couples, and whether the therapist's assessment of the problem and approach to treatment make sense to you. Once you begin, give therapy a chance to be helpful. There are few miracle cures. Change requires commitment and is a gradual and often difficult process. Although some people benefit from short-term therapy (fewer than ten sessions), most find the therapeutic process will require 4 months or longer. The role of the therapist is that of a consultant rather than a decision maker. Therapy requires effort on your part, both during the session and at home. Therapy helps to change attitudes, feelings, and behavior. Although it takes courage to seek professional help, therapy can be a tremendous help in assessing and ameliorating individual, relational, and sexual problems.

Appendix B:
Resources: Books, Videos, and Trusted Websites

SUGGESTED READING ON COUPLE SEXUALITY

Holstein, L. (2002). *How to have magnificent sex: The seven dimensions of a vital sexual connection.* New York: Harmony Books.

McCarthy, B., & McCarthy, E. (2009). *Discovering your couple sexual style.* New York: Routledge.

Perel, E. (2006). *Mating in captivity: Reconciling the erotic and the domestic.* New York: HarperCollins.

SUGGESTED READING ON MALE SEXUALITY

McCarthy, B. W., & Metz, M. E., (2008). *Men's sexual health.* New York: Routledge.

Metz, M. E., & McCarthy, B. W. (2003). *Coping with premature ejaculation: Overcome PE, please your partner, and have great sex.* Oakland, CA: New Harbinger.

Metz, M. E., & McCarthy, B. W. (2004). *Coping with erectile dysfunction: How to regain confidence and enjoy great sex*. Oakland, CA: New Harbinger Publications.

Milsten, R., & Slowinski, J. (1999). *The sexual male: Problems and solutions*. New York: W. W. Norton.

Zilbergeld, B. (1999). *The new male sexuality*. New York: Bantam Books.

SUGGESTED READING ON FEMALE SEXUALITY

Boston Women's Health Book Collective, (2005). *Our bodies, ourselves: A new edition for a new era* 4 edition. New York: Touchstone.

Foley, S., Kope, S., & Sugrue, D. (2010). *Sex matters for women: A complete guide to taking care of your sexual self (second edition)*. New York: Guilford.

Heiman, J., & LoPiccolo, J. (1988). *Becoming orgasmic: Women's guide to sexual fulfillment*. New York: Prentice-Hall.

OTHER NOTABLE SEXUALITY READINGS

Fisher, H. (2004). *Why we love*. New York: Henry Holt.

Glass, S. (2003). *Not "just friends."* New York: Free Press.

Joannides, P. (2009). *The guide to getting it on*. West Hollywood, CA: Goofy Foot Press.

Maltz, W. (2001). *The sexual healing journey*. New York: HarperCollins.

McCarthy, B., & McCarthy, E. (2003). *Rekindling desire*. New York: Brunner/Routledge.

Michael, R., Gagnon, J., Laumann, E., & Kolata, G. (1994). *Sex in America: A definitive survey*. New York: Little, Brown.

Snyder, D., Baucom, D., & Gordon, K. (2007). *Getting past the affair*. NY: Guildord Press.

SUGGESTED READING ON RELATIONSHIP SATISFACTION

Chapman, G. (1995). *The five love languages: How to express heartfelt commitment to your mate*. Chicago: Northfield Publishing.

Doherty, W. (2001). *Take back your marriage*. New York: Guilford.

Enright, R.D., (2007). *Forgiveness is a choice*. Washington, DC: American Psychological Association.

Gottman, J., & Silver, N. (2004). *The seven principles for making marriage work*. New York: Crown Publishing.

Johnson S. (2008). *Hold me tight.* Boston: Little-Brown.

Love, P. (2002). *The truth about love.* New York: Simon & Schuster.

Markman, H., Stanley, S., & Blumberg, S. L. (2001). *Fighting for your marriage: Positive steps for preventing divorce and preserving a lasting love.* San Francisco: Jossey-Bass.

McCarthy, B., & McCarthy, E. (2004). *Getting it right the first time: Creating a healthy marriage.* New York: Brunner/Routledge.

McCarthy, B., & McCarthy, E. (2006). *Getting it right this time.* New York: Routledge.

INTERNET SITES: MENTAL HEALTH

Obsessive Compulsive Foundation: http://www.ocfoundation.org/

National Institutes of Mental Health (NIMH) home page: http://www.nimh.nih.gov/

NIMH, Anxiety: http://www.nimh.nih.gov/anxiety/anxietymenu.cfm

NIMH, Depression: http://www.nimh.nih.gov/publicat/depressionmenu.cfm

INTERNET SITES: HEALTH

National Institutes of Health (NIH): http://www.nih.gov

National Institute on Alcohol Abuse and Alcoholism: http://www.niaaa.nih.gov

WebMD—for many illnesses, including diabetes, cancer, heart disease: http://www.webmd.com

VIDEOTAPES: SEXUAL ENRICHMENT

Holstein, L. (2001). *Magnificent lovemaking.* (Available from the Sinclair Institute, P.O. Box 8865, Chapel Hill, NC 27515; 800-955-0888).

Holstein, L. (1991). *Sex: A lifelong pleasure series.* (Available from the Sinclair Institute, P.O. Box8865, Chapel Hill, NC 27515; 800-955-0888).

Sommers, F. *The great sex video series.* (Available from Pathway Productions, Inc., 360 Bloor Street West, Suite 407A, Toronto, Canada M5S 1X1).

Stubbs, K.R. (1995). *The couples guide to great sex over 40*, vols. 1 and 2. (Available from the Sinclair Institute, P.O. Box 8865, Chapel Hill, NC 27515; 800-955-0888).

Stubbs, K. R. (1994). *Erotic massage.* (Available from the Secret Garden, P.O. Box 67, Larkspur, CA 94977).

The Sinclair Institute. Obtain their catalog from the Sinclair Institute, P.O. Box 8865, Chapel Hill, NC 27515; 800-955-0888; www.sinclairinstitute.com

Sex Smart Films: Promoting Sexual Literacy. *www. sex.smartfilms.com*

PROFESSIONAL ASSOCIATIONS

American Association for Marriage and Family Therapy (AAMFT): 112 South Alfred Street, Alexandria, VA 22314-3061. Phone (703) 838-9808, Fax (703) 838-9805. www.therapistlocator.net

American Association of Sex Educators, Counselors, and Therapists (AASECT): P.O. Box 54388, Richmond, VA 23220-0488, 800-644-3288. www.aasect.org

Association for Behavioral & Cognitive Therapies (ABCT): 305 Seventh Avenue, New York, NY 10001-6008. Phone (212) 647-1890, www.abct.org

Sex Information and Education Council of the United States (SIECUS): 130 West 42nd Street, Suite 350, New York, NY 10036. Phone (212) 819-7990, Fax (212) 819-9776, www.seicus.org

Smart Marriages—the coalition for Marriage, Family, and Couple Education: www.SmartMarraiges.com

Society for Scientific Study of Sexuality (SSSS): P.O. Box 416, Allentown, PA 18105-0416. Phone (610) 530-2483, Fax (610) 530-2485; e-mail: thesociety@sexscience.org

Society for Sex Therapy and Research (SSTAR): www.sstarnet.org

SEX BOOKS, VIDEOS, AND "TOYS"

Good Vibrations Mail Order: 938 Howard Street, Suite 101, San Francisco, CA 94110. Phone (800) 289-8423, Fax (415) 974-8990, www.goodvibes.com

The Sinclair Institute has a wide variety of sex-healthy resources. Obtain their catalog from the Sinclair Institute, P.O. Box 8865, Chapel Hill, NC 27515; 800-955-0888. www.sinclairinstitute.com

Request for Feedback and How to Reach Us

We are interested in your reactions to this book, especially

- What did you find most helpful?
- What was least helpful?
- What could we have addressed more fully?

Please feel free to email or phone us with your comments, requests for workshops or speaking, and questions:

Michael E. Metz, Ph.D.
Meta Associates
821 Raymond Avenue, Suite 440
St. Paul, MN 55114
651-642-9317 x107
www.MichaelMetzPhD.com

Barry W. McCarthy, Ph.D.
Washington Psychological Center
5225 Wisconsin Avenue, NW, Suite 513
Washington, DC 20015
202-364-1575 ex. 6
McCarthy160@comcast.net